STILL STANDING

A LIFE OF PAIN, ADVERSITY AND PERSEVERANCE

JAMES COOPER

outskirts press

Outskirts Press, Inc.
http://www.outskirtspress.com

ISBN: 978-1-9772-0506-3

Cover Photo © 2019 James Cooper. All rights reserved - used with permission.

Outskirts Press and the "OP" logo are trademarks belonging to Outskirts Press, Inc.

PRINTED IN THE UNITED STATES OF AMERICA

This book is dedicated to:

*My brother, **George Allen Walker Jr.** may you rest, in peace. I love you dog, I think about you every day. I will never stop mourning you. I look forward to the day, we meet again, in Heaven. God willing!*

*To my kids: **Jayda Nicole Cooper**, **Javon Allen Cooper**, and **Jerin Domonick Cooper**. You guys are the reason I get up every day. You are what I live for. I love you guys more than life itself.*

Table of Contents

Introduction

IN THIS BOOK, I am going to share information I have kept to myself my entire life. I am going to let you hear my story, visualize my struggles, and take this ride with me. I am also going to explain how I overcame the toughest obstacles in my life. I have included my most fulfilling moments such as: the birth of my kids, graduating college, and signing a contract to play professional basketball. I have also included the most painful moments of my life in situations such as: my mother being locked up, me and my siblings being split up, living without utilities as a kid, the pressure that came with being a local basketball star, and a pain unimaginable, losing my one and only brother. I hope you are ready for this ride. Here we go…

At an early age, I realized I was brought into this world to be different. God blessed me with a unique mind to want to do things my way. I refused to follow behind anyone else, especially if they were doing things I did not agree with. I was going to do it my way. I didn't care about fitting in. As I had gotten older, I would actually become irritated with people who followed others.

I also realized that I didn't think like anyone in my family. Me having a different mentality made it challenging to live under the same roof. Our differences led to many arguments and disagreements. But as I had gotten older, I learned to distance myself to avoid confrontation. So I made it a habit to stay away from home as much as possible. Getting away gave me the break I needed to help keep my sanity. Otherwise, the everyday fighting would've driven me crazy.

I also realized that I was a very impatient person. I wanted things to work the way I imagined it and I wanted it to happen right away. At the same time, I was blessed with a strong mind. I was blessed with a sense of determination. Giving up was never an option no matter what I was dealing with. When I put those two characteristics together I became obsessed with making progress in whatever I was involved with. I had to find a way to succeed, I just had to. I knew in my mind that I would try until I found a way to be successful.

Instead of rushing into things, I would take time to think about whatever I was trying to accomplish. Then I would create a plan to deal with the obstacle. It was the only way I knew how to deal with problems in my life. Looking back, I don't think I would have made it through, if God had not made me the way I am. I survived by carefully thinking and analyzing situations around me.

At a young age, I learned that adversity would be a big factor in my life. I also realized that I would have to find a way to overcome things on my own. I wasn't blessed with a mentor or a positive role model to point me in the right direction. Instead I was placed in a hostile environment filled with drugs, violence, and negative people.

I had to find my own ways to deal with problems in my life. I started by using my own mistakes to help me grow as a person. I wasn't afraid to criticize myself. I wasn't afraid to own up to my own flaws. Whenever I made a decision that affected me in a negative way, I thought about how I could've handled it differently. From there I worked on my plan to avoid making that same mistake. But I didn't stop there. I also watched the outcome of other people's mistakes and tried to avoid going the same route. Adopting this method saved me from a lot of trouble.

Life was rough to say the least. And to make it worse I grew up in an environment where nobody felt sorry for you. Nobody cared. Some people seemed to even enjoy watching other people go through trials. At that point I learned that I had a choice to either fight to survive or allow my problems to control my life. Those were my only options. It was a tough task to complete, but I told myself I would not stop until I figured it out.

I helped my situation by spending a lot of time thinking about my life and how I wanted to live. I didn't have a specific plan at that point, but I knew the way I was living as a kid was no way to live life. I didn't want to live in chaos. I didn't want to be surrounded by drama. And I definitely didn't want to be surrounded by angry, unsuccessful people. People who wanted to drag everyone else down with them.

So, I thought of ways I could give myself a chance to be successful in life. Ways to avoid the lifestyle I was raised in. Ways to avoid the troubles people around me were facing. That was my ultimate goal in life. To live peacefully, be successful at whatever I was involved in, and avoid drama as much as possible.

Thankfully God is all-knowing and He knew the struggles I was going to face. The strong mind He blessed me with was my main source of strength. I was blessed with a mind that would not allow me to give up. I thought it was weak to follow others and make excuses to do bad things. The situations I was exposed to at a young age were anything but normal. But still I refused to feel bad for myself. I had to find a way out. A way to get away from the lifestyle I was born into. I knew I still had a chance to overcome those things. It was up to me to make something out of my life. I also knew that the choices I made would dictate everything.

Rough Start

I was born February 1st, 1986 to Kelly Garrett and James Cooper. That in itself was a problem because I later found out that James Cooper was not my biological father. I was named after him, but I grew up thinking George Walker was my father. Then I ended up meeting my biological father, Marcus Kelley when I was thirteen.

I was named after James Cooper, but I rarely saw him as a kid. The only thing I remember about James Cooper, was he and my mom fighting over me in the *Robinson Drive* projects. I remember he had my legs and my mom was pulling on my arms. George Walker had been around since I was a small child, so he was the father figure I had known. Being around George so much made it even more confusing when I finally met my biological father. The whole situation of trying to figure out who my father was, was very frustrating. It was also hurtful. It caused a lot of self esteem issues for me. I grew up thinking three different men were my father.

I was born the oldest of seven children: five girls and two boys. My mom had me, five girls in a row, and then my brother George was born last. My siblings' names are: Heather, Vashawna, Kyera, George-Ann, Darrien, and George Junior. On my dad's side I have a younger sister named Page. Despite me being the oldest of a large family, none of my other siblings shared the same mother and father as I did. I was the odd man out.

My Escape

When I was a year old I developed a strong passion for the game of basketball. Making shots on my little basket, made me feel good. It was something about seeing the ball go through the hoop that excited me. I became so obsessed that my mom used to have to force me to come in the house after shooting on my *Little Tikes* court. And when she forced me to come in, I would cry because I still wanted to practice.

Sometimes, I would practice shooting on my court up until ten o'clock at night. I was blessed with a high sense of determination at a very young age. Or maybe I was just obsessed with basketball. Either way I found a hobby and I was determined to excel at it.

As a kid there was always a lot of drama in my home. Someone yelling, people arguing, something getting broken, doors slamming, just chaos every day. When I practiced, I was able to get a break and only focus on playing ball. Basketball was my way of getting away from all the chaos. It was a safe haven for me. Shooting alone at the local park gave me a chance to breathe, a chance to think. Just me, the ball, and the rim. No interruptions, no drama. After a while this became a daily routine. Playing basketball was therapy for me before I had even known what therapy was.

When I was competing on the basketball court I only thought about the game. My only focus was my opponent and what I needed to do to win. Playing basketball was easy compared to the conflicts I faced at home. It was the break I needed. It kept me from losing my mind.

If I had not picked up a basketball, I don't think I would be alive today. There were so many negative activities I could have been drawn into other than basketball. Picking up the ball gave me an alternative to using drugs, trying to sell drugs, or following the wrong crowd and ending up in serious trouble. There was so much going on in my home and in my neighborhood, that I could choose a different negative activity every day of the week.

The worst thing that could come out of basketball, was me improving my skills. It was just the activity I needed to keep me away from the chaos. So, I stuck with it. To make it even better, I was able to translate many valuable life lessons I learned on the basketball court to my personal life.

While on the court I learned how to manage my emotions. It was a tough task to learn, but it was necessary. I had to learn to take the good with the bad. I also had to learn that no matter what I did or how good I did it there was a chance I could fail.

To add to those lessons, I learned that I could not please everyone. Life would be much more manageable if I did my best and focused only on progress. Instead of worrying about the opinions of others. I realized that there would always be someone who would have something negative to say about my progress. There would always be a critic ready to jump on any and every mistake I made. So, instead of trying to be perfect I just continued to work to get better. Progress was my only focus. It didn't matter if it was a small or large amount. If I could see improvement, I was okay with it.

Instead of giving into the negativity, I used it as motivation to be better. Better at anything I was involved in. Better at handling adversity in life. I knew there were people who wanted to see me fail. I even had some of my family talk down to me. But my drive would not allow me to fold. No matter what I was dealing with. I was determined to succeed. Desperate to prove the negative people wrong. That mentality changed the way I looked at life.

The only bad habit I picked up through playing basketball, was withholding my emotions. I was taught to never let my opponent see my frustration. And that it is better to act as if I was not bothered, than to show frustration. To play the game with a strong mind and with good body language.

At that age I took things in a literal sense. So, I tried to do exactly what my coaches told me to do. Being the best player on a varsity basketball team as a 15-year-old teenager, I was taught to never show weakness. In other words, don't let my opponent get to me. No matter what they said. No matter what they tried.

My job was to stay focused and do my part to help my team win. My coaches knew that my opponent would try to do things to get me off my game. They were trying to prepare me for the loud chants and aggressive plays from my opponent. I eventually mastered the habit and it helped me succeed on the court.

I had to learn to block everything out and focus on the game. That focus elevated my performance. At one point, during my sophomore season I was averaging more than twenty-four points per game. I would not have been able to do that if I had not learned to block out the negativity. And to be honest, I was even surprised that I was scoring at that rate.

Even though I had worked extremely hard to improve, I was still amazed at what I had accomplished. However, I quickly learned that with success came critics. In other words, being in the spotlight brought extra, negative attention along with the positive praise.

Now that my face and my name was being displayed in the local newspaper, I was subject to be criticized on how I played the game. People wanted to see what the hype was about and it went two ways. People would be amazed at how I performed and become fans. Or they would create their own image of the player they thought I was and criticize my game. The parents of the kids I played against were the most critical. They were willing to say or do anything to get me off my game.

So, I was taught to counter their tactics by acting as if it didn't bother me. Not getting angry, not reacting to dirty plays, or harsh words. Just a blank stare. No sign of any type of emotion whatsoever.

This forced me to grow up quickly. It wasn't an easy task to accomplish, but I knew it was necessary if I wanted to be successful on the court. If I showed frustration it would affect the way I played in a negative way. Plus, it would give my opponent more incentive to taunt me, seeing that their antics were working.

After years of this concept being drilled in my head, it became second nature for me to hide my true feelings. I became a professional at holding everything in. The problems came when it was time to release my emotions. I honestly didn't know how to express myself. It's normal to show emotion, I am a human being. It is expected. But, I allowed the habit of holding everything in to take over.

I didn't realize how unhealthy it was until I lost my only brother to gun violence. The pain was unbearable, unbelievable. I started to lose my mind because I did not know how to release my emotions. I became delusional, suicidal, and it caused many other psychological problems that I battled for years. If I had been able to express myself and get the help earlier I would most likely be in a better place (mentally) today.

CHAPTER 1

Introduced to the Game

UNFORTUNATELY, BASKETBALL WAS not the only game I was introduced to at a young age. I also became familiar with the drugs crack, cocaine, and marijuana after watching my parents distribute those drugs. Once I learned more about drug distribution I knew it was something I never wanted to be a part of.

I understood that it was fast money. I mean who doesn't want fast, easy money? But, I quickly learned that making fast, easy money from dealing drugs had consequences that came with it. Those consequences were: police watching you, drug addicts, and crazy people, in and out of your house, a possibility of getting robbed, and there was a great chance you would spend some time in prison if you sold drugs.

To make it worse my parents were not discrete about selling drugs. They sold the drugs right in the living room of our home, in broad daylight. People were in and out of the house all throughout the day. And if I noticed at seven years old, our neighbors had to have known what my parents were doing. All it took was for one person to call the police and both of my parents would have been put in prison.

I quickly became aware of my surroundings because of the environment I was raised in. I felt like I had to be ready to adapt to anything. I never felt comfortable living in that way. So, I started paying close attention to everything around me. Even the smallest of things. I remembered what the drug users looked like. I remembered what the dealers looked like, the cars they drove, how they dressed, and how they talked. I even remembered most of their names. I also learned what the different types of drugs looked like, how they were bagged, and what the drugs were weighed on.

Those weren't the only things I picked up on about the drug game. I remember my parents discussing getting caught and how they used to act whenever the police came around. I could see the panic in their eyes when they talked about the possible consequences of being caught.

I witnessed a lot at a young age. And I quickly realized that I did not want any part of that kind of lifestyle. I saw what dealing drugs and fast money does to a family. The trouble that came with it and how quickly the money could be taken away.

As kids, my siblings, and I were misguided about the reality of how money was made. We had no clue of how to work to earn an income. We had no clue of what a successful work ethic looked like. We did not understand the value of money. So, even as kids we would waste it on pointless things. We watched our parents get money quickly and spend it quickly, so we spent it quickly. We also were way too focused on material things.

The biggest lesson I learned is when a person distributes drugs they will eventually be caught and put in jail. It's only a matter of time before the police catch on to what you're doing. Both my mom and step dad would later be arrested on drug trafficking charges. That whole situation completely destroyed our family.

My step dad was sent to prison first. It was a shock to everyone in our family. The man of the house was just arrested and sent away. It was a very stressful situation for all of us. Him being sent to prison left us lost trying to figure out how to adjust to life without a man present. I remember my mom telling me that I would have to step in and be the man of the house. I was only nine-years old when my mom and I had that conversation.

How could I protect a family at nine years old? Especially a family involved in the drug game. To make things worse, I'm sure the local drug dealers had found out that my step dad was in prison. With people knowing there were drugs in the house we were very vulnerable to getting robbed.

Our house was an easy target for anyone looking to steal or rob someone involved in the drug game. But, by the grace of God none of those things happened. Looking back, I now realize why we moved so much once my step dad had been sent to prison. I would bet money that my mom was constantly on the move to prevent our home from getting broken into.

We were never robbed, but there were other consequences my family would face. Consequences that caused even more pain than my step dad being locked away. My mom was no exception to the rules of the drug game, as she too was arrested four years later and sent to jail for drug trafficking.

I was in the eighth grade when my mom was sent away. Her going to jail was much worse for my siblings and me, than it was when my step dad was sent away. When my step-father went to jail we still had my mom. But, my parents split up after my step-father was released from prison.

After they broke up he rarely came around anymore. It was just me, my mom, and my younger siblings. So, when my mom went to jail, my siblings and I were all split up. With no adult in our home we were forced to live with whoever would take us in. Otherwise children services would step in and make things much worse. And if children services had stepped in, they would not have allowed all of us to live together. I can't imagine a family being willing to take in a family of seven kids. So staying with family was the best option.

After my mom was sent away, I had siblings living in Springfield, Dayton, and even Trotwood. It was very difficult living without seeing my brother and sisters. We were supposed to grow up together. We were supposed to be living under the same roof. But because our parents decided to participate in distributing drugs, everything was chaotic. None of that would have happened if my parents had worked regular jobs.

Game of Basketball

Basketball was more than a game for me. It always has been and it always will be. I know God put the ball in my hands for a bigger purpose than playing the game itself. It makes it even more obvious that I started playing at such a young age. As I got older, I used basketball to steer me away from the negativity I was surrounded by.

Playing basketball allowed me to get a positive break from the reality of growing up in a rough home. Instead of following the footsteps of my step-father and being irresponsible, I chose a positive alternative. I chose to play ball and release my frustration on my opponent rather than getting involved in detrimental activities.

When I had turned eight, I decided I was going to stay away from home as much as possible. A typical day at home consisted of people arguing, being surrounded by strange people coming to buy drugs, being yelled at, and any kind of drama you could think of. I lived in a chaotic household and I hated it. Literally. So, to keep from going crazy I would grab my basketball, get on my bike, and ride to Sherman Park to go shoot by myself.

I really enjoyed being alone because it was the only time I was able to find peace. The troubles at home were too much to deal with on a daily basis. I learned that I could avoid drama if I avoided certain people and certain situations. When I was at the park I could shoot around for as long as I wanted without any type of negative interruptions. I could also take time to think. To relax.

I made it a habit to stay there until I felt better. The pain I was dealing with was unbearable. Every day I tried to think of ways to get away from my troubles. It was too much to take on. I wanted to cry, I wanted to run away, but I had nowhere to go, nobody to turn to. So, I bottled my frustrations up and continued to use my coping method of playing ball every day.

I hated my life. And after dealing with so much I had lost all hope of living a decent life. Living in a normal home. A home full of love. Surrounded by nice people. People who really cared about me. The only thing I felt normal about was playing basketball. At times I felt like it was my only purpose on earth. The only reason I was alive. If I didn't have basketball, I was pretty much worthless.

Basketball was more than a coping method. There were many other positive aspects that came with practicing so much. One, it helped my self-esteem. Seeing the ball go through the net consistently made me feel like I was accomplishing something. And with continuous practice and improvement, other people began to notice. Older basketball players were amazed at how well I could shoot the ball. Especially with me being so young. Hearing grown men give me praise for how well I could play made me feel good about myself. I felt like I was somebody. I felt like I was important. Like I was being accepted.

I first began playing with the grown men when I was nine years old. Playing against the kids in my neighborhood was a waste of time because I could beat them so easily. So, I played with the adults to give myself a challenge. With the adults being bigger, stronger and more advanced, I had to work harder to score against them.

I became obsessed with playing ball after spending so much time at the park. The problem was basketball was my only outlet. It was the only thing I was good at. So, if I did not perform well on the court I felt even worse about myself afterwards. I would allow my bad performance to carry over into my personal life. Then to make things worse, I would have to go back home.

I got in trouble in school regularly. Not because I wanted attention, but it was my way of letting out my frustration. It didn't help that I went to school at Lagonda. Lagonda was a school located on the north side of Springfield. There weren't many African American students there. With us being the minority, I was called "nigger" on a few occasions. That, along with me already being frustrated with my home life, pushed me over the edge.

Getting in trouble in school was strange because I really liked school. I liked doing my school work. I liked working to earn my grades. Doing school work made me feel like I was accomplishing something. But even though I liked school I rarely spoke because of my self-esteem issues.

But overall, I felt safe in the school environment. Plus, it was another distraction from home. Just not as pleasant as basketball. It helped that the teachers were nice. I really felt like they cared about me. I didn't have many friends in school though. Being quiet made it difficult to make friends. And the few times that I did talk, it was always about basketball. That was the only thing I felt comfortable talking about.

Otherwise, I only talked when I was forced to. My teachers figured out that allowing me to talk about basketball, was the best way to get me to open up. With my behaviors being unruly my teachers discovered a way to help me stay on track. So, they made a deal with me.

The deal was, if I went the whole day without getting in trouble they allowed me to go to the gym for 20 minutes to shoot around. So, every time I had a good day I was allowed to play ball during the last period of the day. I was extremely excited to have another opportunity to play basketball. That deal changed my behaviors drastically. It was just the motivation I needed. More basketball. More time on the court. From that point on my behaviors were better on a consistent basis.

Organized Basketball

As mentioned earlier, I had been known for playing basketball in local parks. But, I had no experience playing for a team in an organized league. I had no idea what it was like to play in front of a crowd, or how to play with referees. The whole experience was intimidating. The gyms would be very loud. There were coaches yelling, the referees blowing their whistles, and parents screaming instructions from the sideline.

It felt like being in my home. A bunch of screaming, yelling, and aggressive people. So, as you can imagine my first year of playing organized basketball did not go well at all. And to make it worse, my step father decided to sign me up for the nine-year old league even though I was only seven years old. Looking back, I can't believe he signed me up to play against kids two years older than me, in my first season of organized basketball. That was a terrible decision!

I was nowhere near ready to play with nine-year-old's in an organized setting. I was behind both mentally and physically. The older boys were much bigger and more aggressive than I was. Plus, they had more experience playing in that environment. With it being my first year, I was too afraid to even shoot the ball. I quickly learned that organized ball was much different than playing street ball.

As soon as the defenders came near me I would freeze up. I would pick up my dribble and pass the ball as quickly as I could. I was so afraid that I did not attempt a single shot the entire season. There was a line the older players were not allowed to cross to give smaller players a chance to breathe. Needless to say, I stayed behind that line the entire season.

Initially, I felt as if that season was bad for my confidence. After the season was over I began to think organized basketball wasn't for me. I was ready to give up. I was angry at myself for not taking a single shot the entire season.

However, that terrible season motivated me to work hard to get better results. That was the point in my life where I became critical of myself. I didn't realize it at the time but criticizing myself would help me in the long run. At the same time, I was too hard on myself. Most people would have gotten the same result in that situation, being that I was playing my first year of organized ball with kids who were two years older than me.

I eventually learned how to turn personal disappointments into self-motivation. From there I turned that motivation into an obsession. An obsession to become a better player. To work twice as hard to reach my goals and conquer my fears of playing against bigger players, in a crowded gym.

I did not realize until later, but that season would influence me for the rest of my life. From that point on, whenever I failed at something I confronted myself. I was honest with myself about my performance and how bad I thought I played. From there, I worked angrily to come out and play better the next time.

That unsuccessful experience would turn out to be the foundation for future success. As soon as that terrible season was over I started my path to redemption on the basketball court. I found out that I wasn't supposed to be playing in the league in the first place. My step father broke the rules by putting a seven-year-old in a nine-year-old league. But, either way I was going to be ready the next time I played organized ball.

I had to wait a year until I was allowed to play organized basketball again. I used that year to work on my skills and prepare myself for the next season. I was determined to be ready the next time I stepped on the court. I started to practice harder than I had ever practiced before. My goal was to be prepared for anyone. No matter how big, strong, or fast they were. I was going to be ready. And I was going to overcome any challenge that came my way.

Time to Redeem Myself

I returned back to the court with a chip on my shoulder. I had something to prove. That season would be my chance to redeem myself and prove that I could play with anybody, in any environment. Success was the only option. Dominating the competition was the only thing on my mind.

I thought about that horrible season the whole time I was in practice. I was anxious to get on the court. I was anxious to start the game. I just had to prove that I was a better player then what I had displayed during my first season of organized basketball.

At age nine, I was allowed to play for my school's team. Every elementary school had at least one team in the league. It was called "Parks and recreation Youth league." My step dad ended up coaching us again. I remember getting custom jerseys and our team name being Michigan. To make it better, my parents bought me the Air Jordan elevens! They were white and sky blue with patented leather.

To this day those are still my favorite shoes. I was so happy to have those shoes, that I slept with them beside me for a week. Having those shoes gave me an extra boost to my confidence. I felt like I could play like Michael Jordan when I wore them.

Our first scrimmage game was on our home floor against a team called the Cougars. I couldn't wait to start the game. This was the moment I had been waiting for. I had practiced alone at the park for two years, waiting to redeem myself. There was no way I was going to allow myself to have another horrible season. That one bad season in the YMCA league was more than enough embarrassment for me.

Gametime!

As soon as coach handed me the ball I came out with a burst of energy. The time to perform had arrived and I was going for it. In my mind I was seeing red. I wanted to completely destroy my opponent. I made my first shot and my confidence grew from there. It made it easier, considering I was playing against kids who were my size. I felt much more comfortable. I was more confident.

I remember keeping track of how many shots I had made during the scrimmage. I counted seventeen made shots in my head as we played the game. I then proudly told my step-dad how many shots I made during our ride home. That type of performance was just what I needed. Especially after playing so timidly during my first season of organized ball.

That scrimmage game influenced my entire season. From there, I went on to lead my team in scoring and to an undefeated season. I had scored at least fourteen points in every game of the season. I rarely ever passed the ball though lol. Still, it was a great feeling to have people come up to me after games telling my parents that I was a good player. It felt great to have such a good season after playing so badly during my first year. I felt like I redeemed myself. It made it even better that our team had gone undefeated that year.

Drugs Taking Over My Home Life

Things on the basketball court could not have been better. I had just led my team to an undefeated season, and I had proved that I could play organized basketball at a high level. My life couldn't have been better. At that age, school and basketball was everything to me.

But life at home was steadily getting worse. At my home in Sherman Court apartments, people were still running in and out of the house for all the wrong reasons. My parents were still selling drugs and our house remained chaotic. There was never a quiet moment in my family's home. Looking back, I don't understand how anyone could live that way. A home is supposed to be a place where you can get away from chaos in the world. A place you can breathe. Relax. Our home was just the opposite.

I knew way too much about the drugs and how they were sold. At the age of seven I became familiar with what a triple beam scale was and what it was used for. I figured out that it was used to measure and weigh the crack rock that was being distributed. It was then distributed to either the drug user or the buyer who would later sell it to their own clients. I became so familiar with the crack game that I caught on to the slang words after hearing my parents and their friends use them so much.

I learned what it meant to be "fleeced" (when a person gives the drug dealer something that looks like the drug but is not actually the drug). I knew the size and terms of a dime bag, a quarter ounce, and many other slang terms used in the drug game.

I heard my parents discuss stories about other drug dealers and what happened in their business. I also became familiar with the regulars my parents dealt with. I knew most of them on a first name basis. Some of them were my older cousins on both my mom and my father's sides of the family. I was stressed but I was also relieved that my younger siblings were still too young to understand what was going on.

I knew the consequences that came with selling drugs, and my biggest fear was my mom being caught by the police and locked away. Sometimes I would envision coming home from school and my house being surrounded with police cars. I began to worry about my parents going to prison every day. Especially my mom.

When she would go to the grocery store I would sit by my window and wait for her to come home. It usually took a while for her to get back. After she was gone for about thirty minutes I would think to myself that she had been locked away. I would nearly be in tears sitting, waiting by my bedroom window. Not realizing that it would take a while to go grocery shopping for seven children. I guess you can say I was paranoid at a young age.

I didn't feel the same love for my step-father as I did for my mother. I had many reasons to love my mother more. However, the main reason I loved my mom more is because my step-father used to fight my mom. I felt bad for my mother for having to put up with a man like that. It made me feel worse that I was too young, and too small to be able to do anything to help my mom.

To this day, I still remember the things my step-father did to my mother. On one occasion, my step-father had told my mom that he would kill her the way her best friend Teresa was killed. (Teresa was beaten to death with a billy club by her boyfriend) I'm still waiting for the day I can repay my step-father for the pain he caused my mom, and my younger siblings. I held in the anger and frustration for years never telling anybody what we had gone through.

CHAPTER 2

Man of the House

ONE MORNING, I was awakened by my mom crying. To wake up to something like that made me nervous. I was afraid before she had even told me what was going on. I didn't know what to expect. I didn't know what to say or what to ask. So, I figured I would sit and wait until she was ready to talk.

After about an hour of crying, my mom told me the bad news. My step-father had been set up by one of his customers and arrested for trafficking drugs. Even though I anticipated my parents being caught by the police, it was extremely difficult to accept the fact that it happened.

When I first heard the news, I was numb. I did not know what to feel or what to think. I was terrified. I began to think to myself: "Who was going to protect us? Who is going to provide for us? What if someone comes in the house to harm us?" Those were just a few of many crazy thoughts that were running through my mind.

Not long after my mom told me what happened, she got on the phone and began calling our family telling them the terrible news. That situation ruined my entire day, my entire week. All I could think about was my step-father being locked up and how much danger we were in. Time seemed to drag by very slowly that day. I couldn't stop thinking about what had just happened.

Later that night my mom called me downstairs to the living room after my younger siblings had fallen asleep. She was still upset about my step-father being arrested, as I could see the tears in her eyes. She sighed, sat there for a moment then told me that I would have to be the man of the house. As soon as she said that, instant fear shot through my entire body.

I had no idea of how I was going to manage being the man of the house. I was only nine years old! I could barely take care of myself not to mention protect a family. I felt fear, a lot of fear, but with the fear I also felt anger. I was angry at both of my parents for putting me in that situation. How could they expect me to be able to handle that?

But even though I was angry, I had to put my feelings aside. I had to find a way to hide my fear from my younger siblings. I had no idea of how I was going to pull this off, but I had to find a way. I was so over-whelmed about the situation that I wasn't able to sleep that night.

I remember going to school even more scared than I was before. Worrying if my mom was okay. Wondering who would protect her while I was at school. The problems I was facing at home were begin-ning to disrupt my entire life. And even though I was scared out of my mind, I wouldn't allow myself to talk to anyone about my home life. I was embarrassed and I was afraid I would get in trouble if I told anyone about our situation. I imagined the school administration would ques-tion my mom's parenting. Then they would judge my family. So, I kept everything to myself.

Not long after my step father was locked up we were piled up in the car, traveling to see him in prison. He was locked up in Lancaster, Ohio, about an hour away from Springfield. It seemed like the drive took days for us to get there, with the car being crowded. It was my first time ever being inside a prison.

It felt strange for some reason. I could tell it wasn't a pleasant place to be from the moment I walked in there. Seeing all the security guards, the locked doors, and the glass screens we had to communicate through. I also noticed that not a single person in the registration department was smiling. Everyone was so serious. So stiff.

When my step-father came out to see everyone he was hardly rec-ognizable. He was forced to shave all of his facial hair and he had lost a lot of weight. I remember the prison guard yelling at the prisoners as if they were in the military. And in response, the prisoners had to respond as a group yelling "Yes sir" to the guard.

Once they were finished talking to the guard they were released individually to speak with their families. It was a strange conversation talking to my step father in that environment. It just didn't feel right.

I later found out that my step-father took a plea to enter the prison boot camp. By entering the plea and completing the program he would get his sentence reduced. The program was designed to be tougher than prison. The guards put them through intense training that required discipline, in exchange for less time. They were also required to participate in many strenuous activities while in boot camp.

Believe it or not, our home life had become even more complicated after my step-father was sent to prison. We began to move frequently once he was sent away. It seemed like we were changing locations every other month! All that moving made me feel uncomfortable. There was no stability in our home and we never really settled into a place. Things had always been chaotic at home, even when my father was there, but the chaos seemed to become much worse with him being locked away. I never felt comfortable during those times. I was afraid and also stressed.

It didn't help that we were moving back and forth to both sides of town on a monthly basis. I remember going to three different elementary schools in five years. In kindergarten, I attended Lincoln elementary, I then transferred to Fulton and stayed there until the second grade. After two years there, I relocated to Lagonda, and stayed there until I was in the fourth grade. Then, I transferred back to Lincoln to finish my fifth-grade year.

Believe it or not, I attended three middle schools in three different states! I started out at Hayward in the 6th grade in Springfield, I transferred to Dwight Rich in Lansing, Michigan when I was living with my dad, and I spent two weeks at a school in Louisville, Kentucky.

I really didn't like moving. I hated being the new kid in school. I had to make new friends, get familiar with a new school, and try fit in with people I had never seen before. And the worst part about moving was being forced to introduce myself in front of the entire class.

After experiencing so much trauma at a young age, I developed low self-esteem. I was very uncomfortable speaking about myself in front of other people. It didn't help that kids usually weren't nice to the new kid in school. The new kids normally sat alone at lunch and didn't have any friends. That was me. I hated changing schools, but it wasn't my decision. So, I had to find a way to get through it.

CHAPTER 3

First Major Loss

THROUGH EVERYTHING THAT went on in my terrible childhood, there was one person I could count on. There was one person I knew cared about me, regardless of what I did. That person was my grandma Quick (my mom's mother). I had never seen my grandma on my biological fathers' side. But, that was okay. In my eyes, I only needed my grandma Quick. She was literally the rock of our family. She was a strong woman who didn't take crap from anybody. But, she had a very gentle side for family and those who were respectful to her.

I really enjoyed spending time at grandma Quicks home. I had some of the best moments of my childhood at my grandma's house. Grandma Quick's home was perfect for me because she did not tolerate any negativity in her house. I also enjoyed being at her house because it was the only time our family acted like a real family. She organized every family gathering and made everyone feel welcome.

We would meet at her house for every major event involving our family. Holidays were always special at Grandma's house. It was such a peaceful environment there. Everyone would be laughing, joking, and telling stories, catching up on old times.

Grandma Quicks' house is where I first met my great-Aunt Margy (her sister), my great-grandma Strodes (her mother), and many other people on my moms' side of the family. They were very friendly, loving people. That side of my family was all about sticking together, being positive, creating a strong upbringing for us.

When we met at grandma Quicks' house the adults would be in the house bonding, talking, and laughing. Reminiscing on the old times. Talking about how everyone has grown up. We (the kids), would be outside in the backyard running around, playing, and being silly. Grandma Quicks' house was the only times I had a chance to play with my cousins. We all really enjoyed being at grandma's house.

I remember my grandma being a fan of basketball. She used to force my uncle Donald (who was eight years older than me), to let me shoot with him and his friends. My uncle would get frustrated, even embarrassed whenever she made him let me shoot with them. But grandma didn't care. I remember her yelling from the back porch telling my uncle to let me shoot the ball one time. I would eagerly run up to my uncle, grab the ball, and shoot. I was excited to take the shot, but I felt pressure as the older kids watched me.

I could tell that my grandma was proud that I wanted to play ball. Grandma would say, "You are going to play for the San Antonio Spurs, and I am going to sit right behind the commentators, and as soon as they say something bad about you I'm going to knock the hell out of them!" The Spurs were my grandma's favorite team because her favorite player, David Robinson played for them.

As mentioned earlier, my grandma Quick was my main source of support. I was her first-born grandchild. I could do no wrong in her eyes. Looking back, I wish I could have spent more time with her. The problem was, I was not old enough to get to her house on my own and she didn't drive. So, my only way of getting to her house was if my mom felt like taking me over there. When I had gotten old enough to go see her on my own, I would ride my bike to her house. But by then my grandma had started to experience health issues.

Regardless of how long we went without talking, we picked up right where we left off. When we interacted with each other you could sense how strong our bond was. I would spend the weekends at her house. It was always fun being over there. It made it even better talking and playing with my uncle Donald and Aunt Quinn. I also had a group of friends I played with who lived in my grandmas' neighborhood. Those were by far the most peaceful moments of my childhood.

Disaster Strikes Again

However, the worst came when I was eleven years old. My grandma had gotten sick. Not the cold or the flu. Really sick. I knew it was serious, because she had gone to the hospital. And as long as I remember, my grandma never went to the hospital. I remember my mom telling me that grandma had suffered from a kidney infection.

At that time, I had no idea of how serious a kidney infection was or what it could do to a person. I just figured it was serious if grandma went to the hospital for it. Grandma ended up staying there for two weeks. But she improved quickly and was sent back home.

As soon as I found out my grandma was released from the hospital, I rode my bike to her house to see her. I was afraid for my grandma when she was in the hospital. At the same time, I was forcing myself to think she would be okay. I desperately wanted to help her. I couldn't imagine my life without my grandma.

When I was riding my bike to her house I began to think of all the positive things my grandma had done for our family. I started reminiscing in my mind about the times she had taken care of me when I was sick. I thought about how she kept our family together. I wanted to do the same for her. I wanted to take her sickness away. I remember going over her house every day for two weeks straight, because I was afraid she would get sick again if I stayed away too long.

After coming home from school one day, my biggest fear became a reality. My mom told me that my grandma was back in the hospital. I instantly began to feel sick to my stomach after hearing the bad news. I couldn't stop thinking about her going away and not coming back. My grandma was irreplaceable. If something happened to her our whole family would suffer. I was scared to point that I lost my appetite.

I then thought about the time Grandma Quick, my uncle Donald, and my Aunt Quinn came to our house banging on the door; screaming and crying when my Great-Grandma Strodes passed away. The pain in their eyes and the looks on their faces is something that I will never forget. I didn't want to go through that again. It was too much to deal with. But I knew it was a possibility after hearing my grandma was back in the hospital.

I was desperate to find a cure for my grandma. And I was willing to do anything to help her get better. It hurt even more when I faced reality and realized that there wasn't much I could do to help. Less than a week after hearing she was back in the hospital, my grandma passed away.

It literally crushed me. I had never cried so much in my life. It was difficult facing the fact that I would never see her again. Grandma Quick passing away really hurt my mom as well. I remember my mom crying for months at a time; trying to cope with the loss of my grandma and raise her kids. As expected, our family was never the same after grandma Quick passed away. The summer before she had passed away was the last time we had gathered together for a holiday.

CHAPTER 4

Unexpected Visitor

AT THE AGE of thirteen I was already a confused individual. I had just started puberty, I had low self-esteem, and I felt like I was only good for playing basketball. To make things worse, I was chubby, I barely had any clothes, and I was being reminded of how poor I was at school every day. The point of saying this is, I didn't need any more negative things in my life.

Well unfortunately, my mom started dating a man that I grew to hate. The situation was so bad that it led to me being sent to my biological father, and us meeting for the first time. My mom dating a guy like Terrance was the worst thing that could have happened to my family. He also, was the worst influence possible for my younger brother and I.

From the moment I met him I didn't like him. He was very loud and arrogant. And to make it worse he gambled a lot, rarely ever winning. Terrance and his friends would shoot dice for money, playing a game called "craps."

He constantly lost money which affected everyone in the family. The money he lost was the money for food and other things we needed. It never seemed to bother him though as he kept gambling and losing. To make matters worse, he would be mad at us after he lost. He would then come home angry, looking to start a fight.

As soon as my mom and Terrance became serious, things began to go downhill. Fast! He wanted to control over everything. Before Terrance, most of my moms' boyfriends were okay. They usually kept away from my siblings and me.

Terrance didn't like for my mom to buy me anything, (not that she bought me much anyway) but whenever she did, it bothered him. I remember my mom buying me a pair of shoes that I did not like. They were funny looking and I knew my friends would make fun of me if I wore them. So, I expressed to my mom that I did not like them.

Rightfully so, my mom was frustrated because I was being ungrateful. In the midst of me and her going back and forth Terrance stepped in. He stepped in, called me an ungrateful punk, took the shoes, and kept them for himself. From there things only got worse.

As mentioned earlier, Terrance had a gambling problem. Well, whenever he lost he would come home angry. He would be angry at us because he had lost his money gambling. From there it went to him fighting my mom.

Whenever Terrance was around our home was in an uproar. The fighting continued to become more and more frequent. My younger siblings really couldn't deal with it. It didn't help that my step-dad disappeared and my mom always allowed Terrance to come back.

It might sound strange, but Terrance was jealous of me. I could never understand why a grown man would be jealous of a thirteen-year old kid, but he was. I noticed his envy whenever someone spoke about me playing basketball. As soon as they mentioned it, Terrance would instantly become angry. I remember Terrance saying I thought I was "all that" after hearing older guys talk about my basketball skills at the park. He really had a problem with people giving me praise. That was sick in my mind. Terrance was an evil, angry person. And after watching him disrupt our entire household, I began to hate Terrance. I hated everything about him. And with that feeling of hatred, I grew less and less afraid of him.

Terrance's' jealousy was a small thing compared to the fights with my mom. I remember a few incidents that almost made me lose my mind. The fights made me angry, but I was more hurt for my younger siblings. They had already gone through the fights between their parents and now they have to deal with him. I was most angry with my mom because she continued to let Terrance come back. No matter what he did she always allowed him to come back.

The first incident was with my sister Heather, the second oldest of our family. Heather was really afraid of Terrance. I knew this because she would cry and tell me how she wanted to run away whenever we were home alone. But every time she talked about running away I talked her out of it. I told her not to because I knew my mom would take Terrance's side and Heather would only get in more trouble.

But one-day mom and Terrance had a fight that scared my sister worse than before. Heather couldn't take it anymore. After the fight, mom and Terrance left the house to go to the store. The second they were out of sight Heather came up to me. She told me that she was scared and that she was really going to run away this time. I tried to talk her out of it, but at the same time I understood her frustration.

After sitting for a while, thinking if she should really do it, she took off running toward the corner. Unfortunately, mom happened to be turning onto our street as Heather had reached the corner. My worst fear had just become a reality. I knew Heather would get in trouble. I was scared for her. But my anger towards my mom overrode my fear for my sister! How could she not understand my sister's frustration? Who wouldn't be scared living in that house with Terrance? Any person in their right mind would completely understand Heather's point of view. But instead of understanding, my mom decided to punish my sister.

My mom punished Heather by giving her a whooping. My anger became stronger as I heard my sister cry after being punished. I remember being so angry with my mom that I did not speak to her for three days. I made sure to avoid all eye contact with my mom. I refused to even look in her direction. I felt like I hated my mom after that incident.

Coincidentally something positive came out of that situation. My sister would eventually get away from Terrance for good. I never figured out what had happened, but I assumed that my sister had told her father what was going on at my moms' house. Heather was already visiting her father every other weekend, but after that incident she never lived with us again. That was the last time me and Heather would ever live in the same house.

Even though me and Heather argued and fought for all those years, I missed her when she left. Missing Heather was weird because our family never expressed those types of emotions. It was strange not seeing Heather at home anymore. And even though I missed my sister, I was happy she was able to get away from Terrance.

Now that Heather was living with her father she would never have to deal with Terrance again. And even though we weren't in the same house, I was able to see her at school. It felt weird not seeing her at home but seeing her at school was better than not seeing her at all.

Another incident occurred with Terrance that would be permanent in my mind for the rest of my life. It really bothered me because it involved my younger brother, George. I was very protective over my little brother. With my step-father being away I was the only male figure in my little brother's life. It was my job to make sure nothing happened to him. I remember being up, unable to sleep, worrying about my brother. Wondering if I could protect him.

The incident occurred when I was thirteen, and Little George was only five. The drama and the chaos in the house really affected my brother. One day, our mom and Terrance had one of their usual fights. All of my siblings were screaming, yelling, and crying. It was a very traumatic experience dealing with the fights every other day.

Again, my brother was only five years old. After seeing so much chaos he developed a habit of running away and hiding when things had gotten bad in our home. It was his way of dealing with the trauma. But after that fight we couldn't find him. We looked everywhere in the house and even outside the house, but still couldn't find him. After more than thirty minutes of looking, everyone began to panic.

I put on my shoes and ran through the neighborhood desperately hoping I would find him. Still, no sign of my brother. Once I returned home I heard yelling in the kitchen. I ran inside and seen that my mom had found my brother hiding inside of the dryer. He was so afraid of Terrance that he had hid in the dryer to get away. I couldn't believe my little brother was actually hiding in the dryer!

I couldn't get that image out of my mind. On the outside my body displayed hurt as tears ran down my face. But on the inside, I felt rage. I knew I had to do something before my mom or one of my siblings ended up getting hurt, or even killed. Just the thought of my brother hiding inside of dryer crushed me. I thought about that for months! From that day forward, I thought about how I would get revenge on Terrance for scaring my brother like that.

That time came about four months later. We had lost our house on Grand and we were living with my moms' friend Jennifer. Terrance and my mom were in front of the house arguing when he had attacked my mom. I remember Terrance trying to physically take money from my mom in the front yard, close to the street. I remember the whole situation like it happened yesterday.

Terrance, and my mom were wrestling over the money. My mom called me to help her. I don't know what made her do it, but she just yelled out my name. She had never done that before, so it really caught me off guard. When she had called me to help all these emotions came running out at once. I felt like I had to do something. I just snapped.

I was fed up with Terrance and everything he had done to my family. A bunch of angry thoughts began to run through my mind. I instantly thought about my sister trying to run away because of him. I thought about my brother hiding in the dryer and I angrily ran towards Terrance. Once I had reached him I just started throwing punches. I used all of the force I had in my body. I ended up hitting him at least three times with a closed fist. I wasn't thinking about his reaction. I didn't care about his reaction. I just wanted him to feel the pain that my family felt. We were all tired of him.

I figured Terrance would try to kill me after I attacked him. But his reaction was more surprising than the situation itself. After I had punched Terrance several times he just got up and walked away. Apparently, the fight scared my mom. I say apparently, because she didn't say anything to me about it, but she called my biological father (who I had never seen or even knew about) to come and get me after the fight. She feared Terrance would come back for revenge.

I met my biological father in the summer of 1999. My family and I were living in Ronez projects with a woman named Terry. To be honest, Terry was a woman my mom sold drugs to, but it was the only place we could go at the time. My mom knew Terrance would not suspect us of staying with Terry. Plus, we did not have any money to get a place of our own. So, all six of us kids, my mom, Terry, and her son were piled up in a two-bedroom apartment. My sister Heather was still living with her father.

I remember sleeping on a small couch with my little brother. It was a terrible way to sleep. The couch was very small. Barely big enough for one person to sleep on, let alone two. But, we didn't have any other option. Plus, it was better than sleeping on the floor.

However, my sleeping conditions were the least of my problems. We were always low on food and the house was overly crowded. Everything we did required a long wait. Sharing one bathroom with nine people was rough. Especially considering the house was built for a family of three. Even trying to watch television, while people continued to walk in front of the television screen was nerve wrecking. As usual, I spent most of my time outside. But there was no basketball court near me so I sat on the steps bored every day.

It also felt weird living with a woman I knew my mom sold drugs to. Times were rough, but at that point I was starting to get used to it. Starting to expect it. There weren't many times in life that I was able to relax, in a normal home. We were constantly living in harsh environments. I was stressed every day wondering what problems the day was going to bring.

One morning, I was awakened by a random knock at the door. I got off the couch half asleep and looked through the peep hole. I didn't recognize who the guy was, so I decided not to open the door. I then ran upstairs and told my mom that there was some strange man knocking at the front door. She came and opened the door and let the man in without hesitation. From there, the situation became strange. After my mom opened the door the man just stood there and stared at me.

It made me uncomfortable as he sat there staring, not saying anything. The awkward silence lasted for about thirty seconds, but it felt like it went on for thirty minutes. I didn't know what to expect or what to say. I definitely wasn't prepared for what my mom was getting ready to tell me. After sitting there watching us stare at each other my mom blurted out "this is your father."

As soon as she said that, my heart started pounding uncontrollably. My mind started racing. I began to feel a hundred emotions at once. I wanted to cry, I felt anger, I wanted to yell. I felt like my mom was lying to me. The feelings of anger and hurt were indescribable. I felt betrayed, I felt lost, confused. I kept asking myself why my mom would lie to me for all those years? How could she keep this from me?

Up until that point I had always thought that George was my dad. Even though he did things that made me question if I was his son or not, in my mind George was my dad. I couldn't believe what I had just heard! I was so shocked at hearing this news that I couldn't move. I just stood there trying to fight the tears. It was a feeling I had never experienced before. All those years I had thought one man was my father, to only find out he wasn't. I was bothered to say the least. I was devastated.

Not only did I just meet a stranger, who happened to be my biological father. But, my mom told me I was going to be living with him in Lansing, Michigan! I couldn't believe it. I continued to sit there. Stunned! I was so angry and confused that I didn't speak. Didn't say a single word. As a stood there I became angry and hurt at the same time. I wondered how my mom could trust that I would be safe living with this strange man. She couldn't have cared about me to put me in that situation. I was hurt beyond words.

I reluctantly went upstairs and started packing up my belongings: three pairs of pants, a pair of shoes, and a couple of shirts. After I finished packing I said bye to my mom and my siblings. Then I got on the road for a five-hour trip to Lansing, Michigan with a person I had never met before. The whole trip was a nightmare.

To add to my frustration, this would be the first time I would travel that far. It would also be the first time I would be away from my family for an extended period of time. Even though my life was horrible I was used to being around my family. It didn't help that I didn't even know how to get back home.

When we finally arrived in Lansing, things got even stranger. I got out of the car trying to gather my thoughts and figure out what just happened. But, before I had gotten a chance to settle in I found out that I had another sister. That was the first time I had met my sister, Page.

Immediately I could also sense that my dads' girlfriend felt funny about me being there. So now I'm living in a new state, with a stranger, and then find out that I have another sister. I was experiencing too many changes at once. It was very overwhelming.

My dad's house was very small. He lived in a one story, half a double with his girlfriend, two kids, and his friend. The house was way overcrowded. Not only were we living in a small area, but we had six people sharing a two-bedroom house. I had to wait in line to brush my teeth and even take a shower. I rarely even had a chance to watch television. And with the house being crowded I was forced to sleep on the couch, yet again. The conditions weren't any better than the way I was living when I was with my mom. Only this time, I was living with a house full of people I had never met.

Not long after arriving in Lansing, my dad took me school shopping because I didn't have any clothes. I immediately noticed the frustration my dad felt about my living conditions in Ohio. My father mentioned my appearance. He also expressed his frustration about me only having three pairs of pants. Especially, considering he paid so much in child support. At that time, I had no idea of what child support was, so hearing him talk about it was foreign to me.

A couple weeks after arriving in Lansing, it was time for me to start school. I didn't know what to expect, but I was extremely nervous. I didn't like the idea of being the new kid in school. I already knew that I would be put on the spot. All eyes would be on me again. I knew the teachers would force me to introduce myself; talk about where I was from, my favorite things to eat, and other things I did not want to share with strangers. I knew the other kids would stare at my clothes, see what type of shoes I wore, and judge my appearance. That's the last thing I needed with my self-esteem already being low. That whole new kid situation made me even more self-conscious. But I knew I didn't have a choice of rather to go to school or not. So I had to find a way to get through it.

There were only four middle schools in the city of Lansing and the city seemed to be a much larger city than Springfield. I attended a school called "Dwight Rich." The middle schools there looked more like high schools, compared to the middle schools back in Springfield.

Even though I hated being the new kid in school, I was excited about trying out for the school's basketball team. I had played against the guys at recess, and I noticed that even though it was a bigger city, they weren't as good as my friends were back home in Springfield. I could score on those guys much easier. Some of the local players didn't like that.

There was one guy in particular who took upon himself to challenge me. I remember him telling people that I was not that good of a player. We ended up playing a heated game of one on one in gym class. Ten to fifteen other students watched while we battled it out. I beat him in a game going to ten. He was still frustrated, but he had to respect me after I had beaten him. It felt good to be able to shut him up.

As usual, it was home where I faced majority of my problems. The school situation wasn't great, but it was nothing compared to what I was facing at home. My dads' girlfriend, Mariah began to express her true feelings about me once my father had gone back to work. She smiled and acted like she was okay with me being there until my dad was no longer around. My father worked second shift, from two in the afternoon until eleven at night. So, I barely seen him during the week. His girlfriend took full advantage of that situation.

Apparently, Mariah had a problem with my mother. She told me how my mom was a bad mother and that my mom didn't do a good job of raising me. This went on for weeks. Weeks turned into months. I tried my best to ignore her comments, but I couldn't hold my tongue forever. I was tired of hearing Mariah talk bad about my mother, so I began to say mean things back to her. But, when my father came home from work, Mariah made it seem like I just started disrespecting her for no reason. With me being a kid, my father took her side without hesitation. He would get angry with me before he even heard my side of the story.

As soon as he would walk through the door, Mariah would be anxiously waiting to tell him about our arguments. It would frustrate my dad, then he would ask me why I argued with her. But, I wouldn't talk to him. At that age I would shut down when I was angry. I didn't want to talk. I just wanted to get away from the drama. So, my dad would make me hold my body in push up position until I started talking to him. After about a month of being there, I started to hate living with them. I hated being in that house. I hated dealing with Mariah and my dad.

Unfortunately, that was only the beginning. My home situation would continue to get worse. The arguments became more frequent. She grew bolder after figuring out that my father would take her side. The drama was starting to break me down. I felt like I was in a prison, trapped where no one could save me. It made it worse that my dad grounded me and I wasn't allowed to leave the house. I was stuck in that house forced to deal with Mariah.

I had to do something to keep my sanity. I had to find a way to get a break from Mariah. So, I began to sit behind the couch to avoid having to deal her. I would stay there for hours every day. It might sound weird, but I felt safe when I was sitting behind the couch. I used to put a cover over my head and sit there all day. I felt like I was in my own space, my own world. No one could bother me if I stayed behind the couch.

But even sitting behind the couch wasn't enough after a while. I really started to hate being there. The drama was beginning to break me down mentally. I was severely depressed and didn't even know it. I was desperate to get away.

Taking Small Steps

So, one day I decided to leave and not go back home. I was supposed to be on punishment, but I didn't care anymore. After leaving the house I told myself that I was not going back to deal with Mariah. I thought about not going back at all.

So, I rode my dads' bike to the park to shoot around by myself. I figured it would help me feel better. But, it wasn't the same as it was when I went to the parks to play in Springfield. Being in an unfamiliar place, and living with someone who did not like me made me feel terrible.

Typically playing basketball took the pain away. Shooting around usually took my mind off of anything I was dealing with. Not this time. I couldn't shake the way I was feeling. I started to feel worthless. I rarely felt good about myself at that point in my life anyway, but living in that house, in those conditions made me feel even worse than before. I felt like I had no way of escaping that situation. I felt hopeless. I was away from my family, in a place I had never been before, living with a woman who could not stand me. To make it worse, my dad did not believe me when I told him what she was doing.

So, I stayed away from the house the entire day. When I finally decided to go back home I laid under a car next door to the house, instead of going inside. I stayed there for hours. Eleven o'clock had past, and my dad had come home from work. I could hear my father talking to Mariah, asking where I was and her telling him she had not seen me. I knew I would get in trouble once my dad returned home, but I didn't care. I hated living there. I was going to fight it as much as possible.

I was already uncomfortable living in a new state. Living with Mariah made the situation even worse. She knew I was pretty much helpless and she took full advantage. I contemplated running away every day after school. But where would I go? How would I get back to Springfield? I was stuck. So, instead of running I was forced to put up with the abuse everyday.

Now or Never

I finally got the courage to fight back after Mariah scared me one day. After one of our arguments she told me that I could no longer eat the food she had cooked. She told me that if I had wanted to eat, then I had to feed myself. That really struck a nerve for me. That reminded me of nights back home when I was not sure if we would have enough food to eat.

There were many nights in Springfield, where I had to act like I wasn't hungry so that my younger siblings could eat. There wasn't enough food for all of us. So, I had to let my siblings eat. Just the thought of not having food again nearly brought me to tears. As soon as Mariah said that I could not eat the food she cooked, I panicked.

My father was at work and wouldn't be home until after eleven that night. So how was I going to eat? I was scared out of my mind. As soon as she finished the sentence, I started thinking of what I could do. My first thought was to look in the couch for loose change. So, I went to the couch and searched in between the cushions to see what I could find. Luckily for me, I found about two dollars in change. I grabbed the changed, then I got on my dads' bike.

I had remembered passing a few restaurants while on my way to school. That made me feel a little better knowing I had some idea of where to go. I figured I would ride my bike until I came across a restaurant that had items I could afford.

I also, had to remember to stay on the main road so I wouldn't get lost. I was so scared and stressed that I was shaking the whole way to the restaurant. My nerves were really bad dealing with that situation. Just the thought of not having food again had me completely shook. But I had to fight through the fear and make something happen.

Through those feelings of being afraid I started to become angry. From that anger came determination. I told myself that I had, had enough and I was going to survive regardless of the circumstances I was living in. I was not going to die in Lansing, Michigan. I used that determination to get on my bike and find a restaurant. I eventually found a restaurant and purchased something to eat; still scared, and unsure of how I was going to survive living that way. At the same time, I felt a sense of accomplishment. I was proud of myself for finding a way to fight back.

Still, that situation with Mariah scared the life out of me. I felt like nothing was guaranteed from that point on. I found myself battling internally about the whole situation. One minute, I wondered how long I could survive living like that. At times, I feared that I would eventually starve to death. Or even worse, end up living with my father and Mariah forever. The next minute I was trying to think of ways I could get away from them. There's no way I could live in that environment much longer. From that day on, I started plotting on ways I could get away from that situation.

Just the thought of not knowing if I was going to eat again, forced me to take action. I sat and thought about what I could do to get away from my dad's house. And after thinking about my options I decided I could write letters to family back home.

The first person I thought of was Mama Rose. (my childhood friend, Josh's mom) I had spent so much time at their house that I knew her address by heart. I planned to tell her about everything that happened at my dad's house. Desperately hoping she would be able to find my mom and get me away from there. I would have written my mom, but I didn't know where she was living at the time. As mentioned earlier, my mom had a habit of moving frequently, so I didn't have a clue of where she was living.

However, thinking about writing letters home and actually doing it where two different things. It was much more complicated than it sounded. The fact that I was only thirteen made the situation even more far fetched. I didn't know anything about mailing a letter, buying a stamp, or any of that. I did however, remember Mama Rose's address. That was a positive start for my situation. So instead of giving up hope I decided to attempt to write her and see if she could help me get back home.

After class one day, I decided to reach out to my science teacher (whom I barely knew) for help with sending the letters home. I didn't tell my teacher anything specific, but I told him I was from Ohio, and I needed to get in contact with my mom. After sending a couple letters home, I could tell that my teacher had started reading my letters before he sent them.

I knew he was reading the letters because he started asking me questions about my personal life. My teacher would wait until class was over, pull me to the side, and ask how everything was going. But I refused to share any information with him. The last thing I needed was another person looking at me funny, another person judging me. So, I continued to act like everything was okay at home.

Despite me sending letters to Mama Rose, the rough days continued at home. Especially when my father left for work. I remember desperately begging God for help. I was anxious to get away from there as quickly as possible. I used to pray that the letters reached my mom. The problem was I had no way of getting confirmation if she had received them or not. So, I had to rely on God and my science teacher.

Fortunately, my prayers would be answered. About a month after I had started sending letters home, God delivered a miracle. I was sitting behind the couch with the cover over my head when I heard a knock at the door. I got up, looked out the window, and couldn't believe what I was seeing! It was my mom! I was filled with so much joy and excitement that I was literally jumping around. I had never been so happy in my life! As soon as I noticed it was my mom I quickly ran through the house and grabbed everything that belonged to me. I wanted to get away from my dad's house as quickly as possible!

Normally, my family didn't show any emotion. Well no other emotion besides anger. But I was so excited to be going home, I couldn't hold it in. I couldn't believe that I would be going back home after all! I packed my things up so fast that I did not even say goodbye. My dad was at work when I had left. I'm sure he was very surprised to come home and find out that I had left back to Ohio. But, I didn't care. I just wanted to get away from there.

All of the sudden life back in Ohio did not seem so bad. I couldn't wait to get home to see my siblings and see my friends. On the way home, I thought about my siblings. I wondered how they looked. How they were doing. How much bigger they had gotten. I couldn't wait to get back home to see them.

I had only lived in Michigan for five and half months, but it felt like I was there five years. There weren't any positive memories about me living there, so it made the time go by really slow. I felt like I had been in prison. Not physically but mentally. Living there, in those conditions hurt my self-esteem even more than what it was before. The only thing I regret was not getting the chance to thank my science teacher for helping me mail the letters home. I felt like he had saved my life. And even though I did not get a chance to thank him personally, I will never forget what he did to help me.

CHAPTER 5

It Can't Get Any Worse

I RETURNED HOME to Springfield a week after basketball tryouts. I was now in the seventh-grade at Hayward middle school. This is when I met Park, (Yelvis Parker) the seventh-grade basketball coach. Park would later have a very big impact on my life.

Initially, Park wouldn't allow me to try out for the team because I arrived after tryouts were completed. Since he had already chosen the players he wanted, he felt it would not be fair to give me a separate tryout. However, my teammates, mainly Isaiah Carson, told Park how good of a shooter I was.

Still reluctant, Park eventually agreed to give me a separate tryout. I was ecstatic to have an opportunity to play for the team. I couldn't imagine missing an entire basketball season. I know I would've been devastated if I had not been able to play. Just the thought of it nearly brought me to tears. But I eventually tried out played well enough to impress Park and he allowed me to join the team.

Although it was a very big deal to be able to play, basketball wasn't the reason me and Park would become close. We developed a bond once Park had become aware of my terrible living conditions. I tried to hide it but Park noticed how I was living. I was always afraid to share personal information with anyone because I was embarrassed. But, my coaches and teachers would always figure it out.

Park caught on to my living conditions after taking me home from practice. It made it even more obvious that I was normally dressed in raggedy clothes. Plus, I rarely had a decent haircut. He also, figured out that neither of my parents were present at my home, so he began to ask questions.

As usual, I tried to avoid the whole conversation. I was too self-conscious to tell Park about my personal life. I was really embarrassed about how I was living compared to other kids on the team. So, I wouldn't talk about my personal life. And even though I knew I needed help I would act like everything was okay. Park was persistent though. He offered me clothes, shoes, a winter coat and even started cutting my hair. That was only the beginning.

Going into the eighth-grade, me and my family were living with our cousin Nancy and her kids. Me, my mom, my siblings, Nancy, and her four kids were all living in a three-bedroom house on Wittenberg. I was forced to sleep on the floor yet again, because the house was so crowded. I made a pallet on the floor with blankets and pillows to make my sleeping conditions bearable. It was uncomfortable, but I had become accustomed to harsh living conditions. Besides, sleeping on the floor would soon be the least of my worries.

Another Blow

After living with Nancy for about three months, one of my biggest fears became a reality. My mom was arrested for drug trafficking and sent to prison! My cousin told me the terrible news the following morning. I remember that horrible feeling of deep depression coming back as soon as she told me what happened. That feeling of hurt, pain, confusion, my mind racing not having a clue of what I was going to do. Having to fend for myself and for my siblings all over again. And at the same time being scared for my mother who was going to prison for the first time in her life.

I remember my cousin Nancy telling me what had happened, the morning after my mom was sent to jail. I also remember her telling me it was okay to cry. And to be honest, I wanted to cry. I wanted to cry as soon as I heard the news. The pain ran deep. So deep that it made my eyes water thinking about everything that was getting ready to take place. But, I wouldn't allow myself to acknowledge the pain in front of anyone. Plus, I knew my younger siblings were watching. And if I broke down, they would follow my lead. So, as usual I held it in. Once again, I had to be strong for them. So, that's what I tried to do.

Multiple emotions ran through my head during that tough time. I was scared for my mom, but angry at my step-father. I was angry with my step-father, because I felt it was his fault my mom had started selling drugs. My mom told me that my step-father taught her everything about the drug game and how it worked.

My mom had never sold a drug before she had met my step-father. And now she is in jail. So, now my mom was locked up and we were without both parents. I was even more scared for my younger siblings though. My step-father had left and only came around once every six months. Now their mom is in jail. But, there was no time for me to complain. I had to figure out what I was going to do, and I had to do it fast.

The bad thing was we barely knew Nancy. And like before, there was drama at her house. I felt like she showed favoritism towards her kids. So, I decided to move me and my siblings' back into our grandpa's house. My grandpa and my aunt Quinn couldn't really help us, but it was a better environment for us. At least we knew who they were.

When my mom had gotten locked away she had left me about five hundred dollars and her car. But we quickly ran out of money and her car ended up getting impounded. My aunt Quinn let her friend, Justine talk her into taking the car to Dayton to meet up with some guy friends. The guys ended up stealing the money and the car ended up getting impounded. So, they came back without the car and lost most of the money my mom had left us.

I was furious to say the least. I was also worried about how we were going to survive without money or a car. How would we buy food? How were we going to transport groceries? The situation was already bad enough and my aunt just made it much worse.

It was very stressful going to school every day trying to focus on schoolwork when we were living that way. I woke up stressed every day, worrying about how we were going to survive. I feared my siblings and I would go hungry. I wondered how we were going to make it. The whole situation was completely out of control.

Not knowing how to fix those situations or how to protect my younger siblings from pain caused extreme stress every single day. I was a walking, nervous wreck. With no money to buy food, and no car to drive to the store, we were forced to move back in with our cousin Nancy. The problem is she couldn't handle six more kids on top of her four kids.

She had to send some of my siblings away with other members of our family. My coward of a step-dad only took one of his five kids, and that was my brother. But Vashawna and Darrien were forced to move to Trotwood with my step-dads' aunt. Me, George-Ann, and Kyera stayed with Nancy. Heather was already living with her father so she was okay.

It crushed me to be separated from my siblings again. I felt it was my job to protect them. How could I protect them if they were living with other people, in other cities? I had no idea of what they were doing or how they were doing. My sisters had never even met their aunt they were going to live with. It was a very bad situation to say the least.

After two months of staying with Nancy I moved away to live with Park, my basketball coach at Hayward. I could not handle the living conditions at my cousin's house. I hated being there. She quickly made it obvious that we were her cousins not her kids. After thinking of who I could stay with I somehow mustered up enough confidence to ask my coach if I could live with him.

Luckily for me, Park agreed to let me stay at his place. Park lived in a small house on the south side of Springfield with his girlfriend, and their son Demond. The upstairs was occupied, so Park made room for me to sleep on the couch, in the basement. .... Back on a couch again.

At that point I had been sleeping on couches for so long that it felt normal to me. I stopped expecting to be able to sleep in a bed. I had no choice but to be grateful for having a place to stay at all. Park definitely did not have to allow me to live in his home.

I was also grateful to be living in a safe environment. A home where I didn't have to worry about drama or being hurt. It helped that there was enough food, and the utilities were on. I felt safe at Parks' house, but at the same time I felt out of place. Me feeling out of place had nothing to do with Park or his family. I just didn't want to step on anyone's toes or be an inconvenience to them. I tried my best to stay out of the way. I wanted Park to know that I appreciated him opening up his home to me. The least I could do was respect his house by not getting in the way.

I sincerely appreciated Park for helping me out. At the same time, my emotions were all over the place. I was trying to settle in at Park's house, but I was also worrying about my family. I was thinking about my mom and hoping she was okay in prison. I was worrying about my siblings hoping they were okay. I wondered if they were safe, if they were eating, how they were doing in school. I thought about all of them daily.

I ended up staying with Park and his family until my mom was released from prison. I appreciated Park opening up his home to me. It really meant a lot. I just felt like I had to go back once my mom was home. I couldn't stay with Park knowing my family was struggling.

When mom got out of prison she brought all of my siblings (except Heather) back to my grandpa's house. Even though the conditions were horrible, I was excited to be living back with my family. I had missed everyone during the six months we were separated.

However, the excitement turned into depression quickly. Going to prison scared my mom away from selling drugs, (which was great in my eyes) so that was no longer an option. She had no choice, but to look for a regular job. But going to prison made it was difficult for her to find a job. Employers were hesitant to hire a person with a felony. My mom went months before she was able to find work.

We would soon face the toughest times we had ever experienced. My mom was forced to move back in with my grandpa because she could not afford a house on her own yet. We had to move back with grandpa because it was the only place we could go. After a month of living back with my grandpa, I realized that the rough times before were nothing compared to what we were about to face.

For starters, we barely had any food. The utilities were constantly being cut off. We didn't have a car after my aunt let my mom's car get impounded. There were even times when we had to boil water and carry the water upstairs to take baths in a plastic bin, because the gas was cut off. Those were very humbling experiences. It was also very, very depressing.

We had rough times before but we had never been that poor. And even though it hurt I had to hide my feelings in front of my family. I didn't want my mom or my younger siblings to see me weak. Seeing me weak would have really discouraged them. But hiding my pain was difficult because the conditions were nearly unbearable. It seemed like every other week something was being cut off. And with no transportation we were really in trouble. Our living situation was very disheartening. I remember going to a room by myself and crying because our living conditions were so bad. It was overbearing to say the least.

One day I went to visit Park and I took a shower at his house without thinking. After living with him I became comfortable in his home. But as soon as I thought about the living situation at my grandpas' house, I instantly felt guilty. How could I take a shower at Parks' house when my mom and younger siblings had to take baths in a storage bin? I felt extremely ashamed about the whole situation. So, I made up my mind to never do that again. If my family was struggling, then I was going to struggle with them.

That year's Christmas was the worst I had ever experienced. I remember receiving only two items. My mom bought me a shirt and a pager. I was frustrated to say the least. Christmas was the time of year when we usually got a lot of gifts, so we all anticipated that holiday coming around. So only receiving two items was out of the norm.

However, my frustration quickly went away when I saw the looks on my younger sibling's faces. You could look at them and tell that they were crushed. What hurt me most was seeing my five-year old brother receive two gifts; seeing my younger sisters get two gifts a piece.

That literally hurt my heart to see the disappointment on their faces. I couldn't stand to look at it. I knew I had to get away before I broke down in front of them. I snuck away, went upstairs to my room and cried. I couldn't believe how bad we were living.

I hated seeing my siblings go without. It made me feel worse that there was nothing I could do to help the situation. I then became angry with my step-dad all over again. I felt like he should've helped. I felt like my step-dad should've stepped up as a man and did more for my younger siblings. But he was more concerned with his new girlfriend and his new family.

Time to Step In

My mom eventually found a job working for a hotel on the east side of Springfield. The hotel company allowed my mom to stay in a room, free of charge while she worked there. She stayed there with her boyfriend while we stayed with our grandpa. With my mom moving out I had to help even more.

I didn't like it, but the pressure motivated me to make sure my siblings were taken care of. I had to stay focused through the tough times and find a way to make it work. I had to make sure my younger siblings got up and was ready for school. Then, I walked them to school. After I made sure they had gotten to school safely, I went to school myself. My biggest fear was letting them walk alone, and something happening to them. So, I made sure I walked them to school every day. It was a very stressful situation altogether.

Things were even worse once school was over. Trying to watch over five younger siblings, with no parent around was a full-time job. A job that definitely wasn't meant for a fourteen-year-old. Plus, we didn't have cable so we had to find other ways to stay occupied. We were forced to play outside all day.

And of course, we were low on food, which was another struggle. I remember cooking food that wasn't fit for kids to be eating. Most of it was expired, but we did not have any other options at the time. We mostly ate canned goods, oatmeal, and boxed foods. The problem is I had no idea how long the items had been sitting in the cabinets. So, I hoped and prayed that everyone would be okay eating it. This went on for about a year.

All the Motivation I Needed!

A year later, we moved back in with my mom. I thought moving back in with my mom, and us being together would be a good thing. But I had quickly forgotten how my mom always seemed irritated with us. She would get bothered so easily over every little thing. So to avoid that stress and drama I stayed away from home as much as possible. I had always hated confrontation and I knew there was a great chance of running into it at home. Staying away was my only answer for dealing with the drama.

I had created a routine to keep my piece of mind. I would go home after basketball practice, run straight up to my room, grab a change of clothes, and walk to the YMCA. If I didn't have practice, I would go straight to the Y from school. I would stay at the Y every night until they closed at 9:45 pm.

Then I would sneak in the house, take a bath, and go to my room. That way I would not have to deal with any drama. It helped that the YMCA was only a couple blocks away from my house. I practically lived there. I figured it was a win-win situation. I would avoid drama while also working on my basketball skills. And I could be alone for a while. Being alone helped me in so many ways. No one could bother me if I was alone. Plus, I could think in peace.

But as expected I couldn't avoid the drama in my home forever. I would try my best to get in and get out, but it didn't always work out. It was very frustrating living like that, but it helped me avoid drama so I continued to do it. Otherwise, my mom would find any and every reason to yell at me. One situation stood out from the rest though.

I had gone home on a Saturday evening. I was in the front room watching television when my mom stormed in. She started going off about me drinking one of her sodas'. I drank one the night before without asking and it really irritated her. I should not have drunk her soda without asking, but I didn't feel like it was that big of a deal. At least not big enough to be screaming in my face.

After seven to eight minutes of trying to ignore her, I got angry and snapped back. I told her it's crazy that she yells at me for every little thing, but she doesn't say anything when her boyfriend has all of his friends in our front room playing the video game. They would be playing the game for hours. Grown men! We couldn't even watch our own television because they were playing the video game all day.

My comments made her even more angry. She stormed off upstairs, grabbed the little bit of clothes I had, put them in a trash bag, and threw them in the front yard. She then came back in and told me to get out of her house. As I was walking out she got in my face and screamed, "YOU WON'T BE ANYTHING BUT A DOPE BOY ANYWAY!"

Angry doesn't even come close to describing how I felt at that moment. I felt hatred for my mom. Real hatred. I was also embarrassed that she had thrown my clothes all over the front yard. I didn't know what I was going to do or where I was going to go. But I had to get away from there.

My feelings were crushed. I wanted to cry, but the anger and my pride wouldn't allow me to shed a tear. Plus, I didn't want to give her the satisfaction that she had hurt me with her words. So, I picked my stuff up, put it in a bag, and started walking toward the corner. Embarrassed, I took the clothes back and placed them on the porch. From there I walked to my coach's house.

I was too ashamed to tell him all the details of what had just taken place. Who would believe that my mom had gone to those extremes over me drinking one of her sodas without asking. So, I just told him that my mom kicked me out and I needed a place to stay. I was fifteen years old and I didn't have a place to stay! Who gets kicked out of their house for drinking a can of soda? I was so embarrassed. So ashamed.

Luckily for me, my coach allowed me to stay at his house. As soon as I arrived I found a quiet place where I could sit alone. I didn't want people to see me in that state of mind. And, I definitely didn't want them asking questions about my situation.

When I had found a quiet place, I sat down and began thinking about everything that had just happened. I was trying to process everything, but it was very difficult because of the extreme emotions I was feeling. I was so angry. I just wanted to lash out. I felt like I needed to unleash my anger. I was holding so much in that I could feel it in my chest. I was also hurt. I wanted to ball up and cry. On top of that I was embarrassed. It took more than a week for me to get over what my mom had done.

I thought about it so much that I stayed in an angry/hurt state of mind for days. After a while that anger turned into motivation. I told myself that I was going to find a way to be decent at whatever I chose to do with my life. And that I would NOT ever sell drugs or be a dope boy. I continued to play my mom's words in my head. "YOU WON'T BE ANYTHING BUT A DOPE BOY! YOU WON'T BE ANYTHING BUT A DOPE BOY!" I couldn't stop thinking about it. I heard it over and over again. Hearing those words was starting to drive me crazy.

So, I made up my mind to fight to work through that situation. And in that time, I decided to write my mom a letter. That was the moment I knew I was going to get into a college. I was going to get into college somehow, some way. I didn't know how I was going to do it. And I wasn't confident at all! But I was not going to allow anyone, not even my own mother, dictate the kind of person I was going to be. No one was going to put limitations on my life!

I included all of those thoughts in the letter I wrote my mom. I remember writing, "I don't know how I'm going to do it, but I am going to go to college. And I am going to graduate. I don't care what you or anybody else has to say. I'm going to do it. And I will never be a dope boy!" I meant every word I put on the paper. Thinking it was the first step. Carrying out those words would be the hard part. Either way I was determined to get into college.

I ended up staying at my coach's house for a week. After those seven days were up, he told me it would be best that I go back home. I completely disagreed with him, but I couldn't force him to allow me to stay in his house. I returned home, but the tension was still there. I was still bothered about what my mom had said to me. Going back was very difficult because I didn't want to be anywhere near my mom. I usually didn't hold onto negative things that long, but that situation was different. She had gone too far.

I told myself from that point on I would find a way to get through every stressful situation. I went back to my plan of staying away from home as much as possible. It was the only way to keep a piece of mind. Looking back, I realize that God had guided me in that situation. I don't think I would've survived if He had not watched over me. He also helped me accomplish my goal of graduating college, eight years later.

CHAPTER **6**

Finding Light in a Dark Situation

AS A YOUNG kid, I recall going to vacation bible school a couple times in the summer. The big, white school bus would come through the Southend projects, pick the kids up, and bring us to the church. I don't remember ever going to church before going to bible school. My family was not involved with church, so that was all new to me.

At bible school we learned about God through coloring, playing games, and memorizing bible verses. This wasn't particularly church, but it was the closest thing to church I would experience until I was old enough to go on my own. Majority of the kids in the bible class thought it was play time. But even at the young age of six I felt different about being there. I wanted to learn more about church. I wanted to learn more about God. The whole atmosphere was something I had never seen before. Plus, the teachers were even nicer than my teachers at school. I loved that environment. The problem was that the program only lasted for the summer.

After the bible school experience, I bounced around from church to church, only going occasionally. However, I finally found a permanent church home when I was thirteen years old. Initially, I was only supposed to go to one service because of an agreement I had made in order to play in a basketball tournament. But once I attended the church I fell in love with it.

I found out about the basketball tournament through Park, after attending the annual church picnic with him. I wasn't interested in going until he told me they were going to be playing basketball. Once we arrived at the picnic I instantly wanted to play. As soon as I had seen the crowd and the heard the balls bouncing I was determined to find a way to get into the tournament.

Whenever there was a basketball game, tournament, or contest I felt like I had to be involved. There was no way I could just walk past a competition without playing. As soon as Park and I walked up to the court I anxiously started asking if I could play in the tournament. Park told me it was okay with him, but it had to be approved by one of the ministers of the church.

I asked Park to point me in the direction of one of the church leaders, so I could ask them if I could play. And as soon as he showed me I quickly ran up to the deacon and asked if I could join the tournament. At first the deacon wouldn't allow it because it was put together for church members only. He said it would not be fair to allow me to play since I was not a member of the church.

I was devastated that he would not allow me to play in the tournament. But, apparently the deacon noticed the pathetic look on my face, so he made a deal with me. The deacon told me that if I agreed to attend church (Greater Grace Temple) that I could play in the tournament.

As soon as he said I could play my face lit up with excitement. I knew I would have to hold my end of the bargain, but I would deal with the church part later. At that moment I just wanted to play basketball.

The tournament turned out to be a blast. It was great to be able to play in such a concentrated environment. If you were passing by you would not have been able to tell it was a church tournament. The games were very intense plus the crowd was into the games. It made the situation even better that I was able to play alongside Park.

Once the tournament was over it was time for me to complete my end of the bargain and attend a church service. Just the thought of being in church with all those people was intimidating. They wore better clothes than me, were smarter than me, and they looked much more sophisticated than I did. I always felt out of place in a church.

Even though I wanted to learn more about God the thought of being in church scared me. I knew from past experience that church members usually dressed nice. Everyone looked so well put together. The idea of being in that environment was very threatening. I barely had any clothes to begin with, not to mention nice clothes.

To make it worse, I never felt good about myself growing up. After noticing how poor I was, and hearing my classmates make jokes about my appearance; I developed a habit of thinking poorly of myself. I tried to avoid large crowds of people as much as possible. I didn't even want to walk into the church because of my self-esteem issues. But I had already given the deacon my word so I had to go.

When I finally got the courage to attend the church, I was so nervous that I walked in with my head down. I then, went directly to the very back of the church. I made sure to sit in a spot to where no one would notice me. I was very nervous to say the least.

But, once I had a chance to hear Pastor Ronald Logan preach, once I had seen Pastor dance, and once I heard the choir sing, I fell in love with Greater Grace. Pastor Logan preached his sermon so that everyone could understand his message. He did not try to use big fancy words to get his point across. He explained it in ways that the average person could understand it. The fact that I could clearly understand his message made me feel comfortable.

I was excited about the opportunity to learn more about God. And I was even more excited to have another place to get away from drama at home. I felt like I was in my own world once I sat in the back of the church. I knew that if I had sat in the back that my chances of being called to the front were very slim. I could sit there and enjoy the service in peace.

I worked through the nervousness and remained a member of Greater Grace. I ended up staying at the church for more than eighteen years! Before that experience I never imagined that going to church would be a routine in my life. Not to mention going for that long. But it was something I wanted to do. Something I needed to do.

Making that decision affected my life in many positive ways. It allowed me to get closer to God. It enabled me to learn more about God and how He wanted me to live. Nobody but God could bring me through the situations I had faced. Going to church also allowed me to grow as a person overall. I am very grateful for that.

CHAPTER 7

Thrown into the Fire

LIFE AT HOME continued to be stressful. For some reason I never seemed to be able to find peace in my personal life. Fortunately, for me I began to experience success on the basketball court. A level of success I had never encountered before. The timing could not have been better.

I was a fifteen-year old, sophomore at Catholic Central High School with barely any varsity experience. And even though I put in a lot of work to get better, I never could have imagined the success I would have on the court that year. I had always dreamed of having a successful basketball career, but dreaming it was the easy part. Putting it into action was much more difficult. And once I started to experience success I fell in love with the rush that came with it.

During my freshman season, I started on the junior varsity team. I didn't play any significant varsity minutes though. Still, I was determined to make more of an impact on the varsity level, during my sophomore year. My team had just lost nine seniors to graduation. That was the perfect time to step up to the plate and show what I could do.

I started by working extremely hard in the weight room. I knew I had to get stronger, otherwise I would get struggle on the varsity level. I also worked hard on improving my skills on the court. I helped my situation by playing a lot of AAU ball over the summer, against some of the best players in the country. That really helped my confidence going against those guys. I knew that if I could challenge the best, then I would be prepared for anything local competition had to offer.

After working on my game and having a great summer of AAU ball, I was anxious to get the season started. And I made it a point to send a message early in the season. A point that I was on a mission to prove that I was one of the best players in the city. However, I had to overcome some trouble early in the season.

I was placed on the bench during opening night. My coach sat me as punishment for playing basketball at the YMCA after practice. It was a team rule that we were not allowed to play street ball during the season. He feared that we would get injured playing street ball, but I went and played anyway. Playing basketball was all I knew so how could my coach expect me not to play? It was very difficult for me to watch a pickup game and not get involved.

Coach not starting me gave me the extra motivation I needed. I was angry that he sat me on the bench because I was forced to watch the start of the game from the sideline. That was very difficult to not be on the floor for the start of the game. I had worked so hard preparing for the season and now that the season had started I was sitting on the bench.

To make it worse, my team fell behind quickly. I anxiously sat there waiting to be called into the game. When coach finally called me to go in, I quickly ran to the scorer's table. I the let my frustration out by scoring within ten seconds of being in the game. From there, I held onto that momentum for the rest of the night. I continued to play aggressively, finishing the game with twenty-nine points. To make it better, I helped my team get the victory. That was the first time I ever scored that many points in an organized game!

After having such a good game, I received my first newspaper article. I also, participated in my first interview with a local sports reporter. All of that was like a dream to me. I couldn't believe I was being featured in the newspaper. It felt great to see my name and face placed in the sports section of the Springfield News and Sun.

However, I had to get over that excitement and get ready for the next game. Our second game would be a bigger test for me and my teammates as we faced Kenton Ridge. Kenton Ridge had just come off a big win over a division one school, Springfield North.

They featured two senior guards who were both averaging over twenty points per game. Andy Shelton and Matt Nienaber were their star players. To make it more challenging, we had to play them on their home court.

It didn't matter to me though. In my mind, I was determined to find a way to help my team win. Coach put me on their best player and I held him far below his average while scoring twenty-one points myself. Holding him below his average and leading my team in scoring helped us win the game. After that game I was featured in another article stating how I was averaging 24.5 points per game and leading the county in scoring as a sophomore.

The morning after the Kenton Ridge game my mom woke me up for school with a big smile on her face. "You won't believe who's in the paper today!" She then flashed the newspaper in front of me. There was a large picture of me in the sports section. The article highlighted how I had led my team to two wins, and that I was scoring at a high rate to only be a sophomore. It felt really good to be recognized in the newspaper. I felt like my hard work was finally paying off. All that time in the weight room, in the gym, and at the local parks had finally come to the light.

I was very happy about the positive attention I was receiving. I would finally be known for being a good basketball player. It was something I had dreamed about since I was a small child. However, I was not ready for the negative aspects that came with being in the spotlight. I quickly learned that everyone did not want to see me succeed. As a fifteen-year-old teenager, I was naive to the realities of being recognized as a local basketball star.

Up until that point I had only thought about the positive facets of being known as a basketball player. I had never even thought about the adversity that would come with receiving so much attention. I was also, not aware of the pressure that came with it. After being put on that platform people began to expect a lot from me. Everything I did was known around the school and around the city. It was something I had to get used to and I had to get used to it quickly.

My wakeup call came after someone had told me about an online message board called, "JJ Huddle." This message board was a place where people would debate about sports topics and local players on-line. I had never even heard of this message board before it was brought to my attention. But I quickly grew to hate it.

Grown adults would get on the site and criticize local athletes. I happened to be the topic of discussion, after I was featured in the two newspaper articles early in the season. Apparently, there were some parents who did not think I should've been featured in those articles. They were saying that I did not deserve that attention.

My confidence was crushed after reading the comments the people posted about me. Just when I felt like things were going well I was reminded of how fast things could go south. I had never experienced anything like that. At that age I wanted everyone to like me, but once I realized they didn't it crushed me.

I instantly went back to my middle school days of feeling hopeless. I felt alone. I felt like there was no way I could overcome the obstacles I was facing. I couldn't talk to my mom about it, and my coaches felt like it wasn't a big deal. It had gotten to me so bad that I thought about quitting so the pressure would go away.

But after a couple days of overthinking the situation, I got back in the gym and continued to work. I figured I would work my way through it. That was the best way to deal with the adversity. The critics weren't going anywhere so it was up to me to shut them up. My plan was to silence them by playing even better.

My sophomore season would turn out to be a season of ups and downs. I didn't like the negative aspects of it, but I learned a lot about life during that season. I quickly learned that adversity is a large factor in life and that everyone had to deal with it. But what mattered most is how I responded to the adversity. From that point on I expected adversity with anything I was involved in. I told myself I would face it head on and overcome whatever came my way.

I had two options when it came to approaching troubles in life. Either let negative people, critics, and my mistakes define me or use the negativity as motivation. I made it up in my mind to use the negativity as motivation. My plan was to think about my own mistakes on the court, and work on them to overcome those mistakes. Adopting that mentality enabled me ignore the negative aspects and focus solely on progress. Nothing else mattered as long as I was making progress.

I was determined to succeed regardless of what anyone had to say about me. I just wasn't mature enough to do it consistently at that time. I had moments where I still let the negative comments and doubters get to me. And at times, I really beat myself up about it.

I later learned to include God in everything I was involved in. I could not figure everything out on my own. I realized that I did not have the answers for life but depending on God made things much easier. When I put my determination together with wisdom of putting things in Gods' hands, I began to figure things out.

At school everyone thought my life was perfect. They assumed that since I was being displayed as a basketball star, that everything was easy for me. Not knowing about my home life or how difficult it was to fight off the negative comments people made about me. They did not understand the pressure I felt stepping on the court every week. Life was anything, but good at that point. But I continued to hide my struggles in front of people. I knew that the more the public knew about me, the more vulnerable I was to being judged. So, I refused to expose anything about my personal life to others.

The negative comments weren't the only forms of adversity I would face during that season. After hearing my name be spoken throughout the community and seeing myself in the newspaper, people began to compare me to other players. People in my neighborhood, on the south side of Springfield began to say I could only play against "white boys" in the county league. They said I couldn't put those numbers up against the competition Springfield South was playing against.

I heard it in barbershops, at the grocery stores, and everywhere I went in my community. Instead of blocking it out and staying focused I let those comments get under my skin. And that affected me in a negative way, in a big game that season. My team played Springfield North (the only division one team on our schedule) that year and I psyched myself out before the game had even started. After hearing so many negative comments from so many people, I began to doubt myself. I began to wonder if the comments they were saying were true. Was I really that good? Or was I only a good player when I played against the county schools?

Needless to say, I had a horrible game against North. I scored a season low, four points and we lost the game on our home court. I only shot the ball a total of five times, because I was afraid to miss a shot. I figured if I had taken less shots there was less of a chance of me missing. I had completely taken myself out of the game. I was so frustrated with myself that I didn't eat after the game that night.

I remember walking through the crowd with my head down desperately wanting to get away. When I had finally gotten home I went straight upstairs and went to sleep. I didn't say a word to anybody. I was so ashamed that I could not hold back the tears of frustration. I already knew what was coming next. All the doubters, and local critics had received just what they wanted. In their eyes that game against North was confirmation that their comments were true.

After that terrible game against North, I had another terrible performance. Psychologically, I had not recovered from the North game. I was still thinking about how bad I played and I let it carry over into the next game. Those back to back bad games really destroyed my confidence. The self-doubt began to grow more and more with me playing so terribly. Unfortunately, those two games were only the beginning of what was to come.

Worst Performance of My Career

Later in that season, I played the worst game of my entire basketball career. And that is saying a lot considering I have played in thousands of organized basketball games. This time it came against one of the worst teams I had ever played against. Triad. This team had not won a game in over two seasons consecutively!

Once again, I let the pressure get to me. Once again, I psyched myself out before the game had even started. In the locker room before the game, my coach explained how the team (Triad) had not won in a long time. He also explained to us that they were desperate for a win. He then said they would be very aggressive, especially towards me. Their goal was to limit my scoring to give them a better chance of winning the game. I was the leading scorer of the team, and if they held me under my average the other guys on my team would panic. And that is exactly how it played out.

Triad's team came out with a lot of energy. Ironically their home crowd had displayed even more energy than the players. Every time they scored the crowd roared as if they had made a game winning shot. I couldn't believe how loud the gym was. Both the fans and the players on the bench were screaming, yelling, and jumping around at every good play the team made. You would've thought it was the state championship game the way they were celebrating.

The team was overly aggressive on the defensive end. Their coach had a great strategy of putting multiple players on me. They face guarded me to prevent me from getting the ball. That forced me to exert energy fighting to get open. Then, once I got the ball, they set up their defense to force me to pass it. There were defenders surrounding my every move. It made it very difficult to get a shot off. Everywhere I went they had two to three defenders waiting for me. They were coming at me so fast that it was tough for me to react. As soon as I got the ball I knew I had to take a quick shot or pass it before they trapped me. It was a very frustrating game.

The crowd, along with the aggressive defenders bothered me. Bothered me to the point where I did not score a single point the entire game! We ended up losing the game allowing Triad to earn their first win in over a year and a half! As soon as the buzzer went off the crowd rushed the floor with excitement. All of their fans ran around the gym smiling, hugging and high-fiving each other.

That was the most embarrassing loss I had ever taken as a basketball player. It is a loss I will never forget. I couldn't believe I had allowed them dictate the game that way. I was devastated. I was embarrassed. I didn't score a single point and we lost!

After having those horrible performances, I somehow managed to fight back and refocus. I had to look myself in the mirror and force myself out of that slump. My only option was to come out the next game with extreme aggression. I was determined to have a better game. The plan worked and it helped my confidence going forward. I finished the game with twenty-two points, in a victory over Cedarville.

I finished the season as the third leading scorer in the area, averaging seventeen points per game. I made first team all-conference, and I also made the all-league, and all county teams. I became the third sophomore in Clark County history to make all county (John Carson and Jason Collier) were the only other sophomores to be all county, and they were legends.

After that year ended I was determined to get better. I thought about every disappointment from that season. I thought about every bad game, every loss. I even thought about all the shots that I missed that I normally make. I thought about how inconsistent I was throughout my sophomore year.

I knew I had to work twice as hard to get prepared for next season. My name was out there and that meant I would face the opposing team's best defender every game. I also knew that my opponent's fans would be coming after me too. I was on a mission to get stronger, and work to improve my skills overall to reach my goals. That summer I worked harder than I had ever worked before.

I played at the YMCA. I played at parks in Springfield. I played with my high school team in shootouts, and I played AAU again. I ended up playing for five different AAU teams throughout the summer. I played basketball every day of the week. Plus, I was on the road traveling nearly every weekend. The constant grind was starting to show in my performance.

I ended up having the best summer of basketball of my career. After performing well in the big tournaments, I was beginning to gain attention of some of the top AAU teams in Ohio. I remember a coach from All-Ohio Red asking me who I played for, after I performed well in a showcase. I felt honored to be asked by the coach of All-Ohio Red. I always wanted to play for them. But, I was already playing for four teams, so there was no way I could work that out.

My Uncle Passing Unexpectedly

As usual, my personal life continued to be rough. There was always something negative going on. It seemed like I could not catch a break at home. One morning my mom woke me up out of my sleep just as she did when I was featured in my first newspaper article. But, this time she wasn't smiling. She had tears in her eyes. As soon as I had seen the look on her face my heart dropped. I could tell that whatever she was going to tell me was not going to be good.

My mom woke me up to tell me that my uncle Donald (my mom's brother) had died suddenly, after having an asthma attack. My uncle was only twenty-four years old when he passed away. To make it worse, we had just seen him the night before. He had stopped by our house to see everyone.

Being woke up to news like that devastated me. It was a terrible way to start the day. I didn't know how to react. I didn't know what to say. I didn't know what to do. That feeling that I hated, instantly came back. That same feeling, I was afraid of. I felt like I was paralyzed. Hurt, confused, and frustrated all at the same time. I hated to see my mom like that. And the thought of never seeing my uncle again cut deep.

After telling me about my uncle, my mom asked me if I still wanted to go to school. At first, I thought I would stay home because I wouldn't want everyone in my business, asking questions. I also knew it would be difficult to hide my emotions in school after hearing what had happened to my uncle. But staying home would've been worse.

So I decided to go to school. I figured it would have been worse sitting at home thinking, about my uncle the entire day. Being at school would give me a short distraction from the situation. That was the one time I felt being around people would be a better option than sitting at home, dwelling on a situation. So, I went to school and acted as if nothing had happened.

I was dying inside, but nobody could tell the difference. After doing it for so long I had become good at hiding my personal problems. It was a very unhealthy habit to develop, but it was the only way I knew to deal with difficulties in my personal life.

It was especially tough with my uncle being so young when he passed away. My family did not have the money to hold a funeral for my uncle. So, we had to cremate his body. We then put together a small memorial service to pay respect to him. The whole situation was very rough to deal with. It really broke me down to see my great aunt Margy crying. Aunt Margy is my grandma's younger sister.

It was rough seeing anyone in my family cry, but it really bothered me to see her crying. Aunt Margy is normally a calm, positive person. She was always smiling, speaking about God. She spoke words of encouragement, words of hope. So to see her break down, made the memorial service much worse. I had never seen her cry, prior to my uncle's memorial service.

To add to my frustration, my sister Heather was also having a hard time dealing with the death of my uncle. I had not seen my sister in over five months, and when I finally did see her again it was at our uncle's memorial. That was a dark moment for me. It took a while to get over losing my uncle. It hurt even more seeing my family hurting like that.

First Time Experiencing Health Issues

Unfortunately, the problems did not stop there. I had grown up in the Springfield City Schools system. They offered free lunch for students whose parents made less than a certain amount of money. With my family's condition, we obviously did not meet the income standards. I had been on the free lunch list my entire life, so the idea of paying for lunch never crossed my mind.

Well things were different at Catholic Central. It was a private school and they did not have programs put in place for students who were below the poverty line. So I needed lunch money for school every day. That was a major problem for me. I hated asking my mom for anything because I knew she would get angry. I tried my best to avoid asking for anything unless I absolutely had to. This situation would seem small for the average person, but it was a major stress for me.

Initially, I refused to ask for lunch money. But to be honest, it was very difficult to go the whole day in school on an empty stomach. So I went ahead and asked my mom for lunch money. I figured the worst she would do was yell and embarrass me. So I told myself I would ask. But even though I told myself I would ask, I put it off for a couple more days. I always hated confrontation. And when I knew there was a chance of it coming, I tried my best to avoid it.

The problem was I needed food to get through the day. I needed food to survive. After about a month of not eating, my stomach started to growl loudly in class. This drew attention to me causing me to feel even worse. So I forced myself to ask my mother for lunch money. And as expected she became very angry. I was so frustrated by her reaction that I told myself that I would not ask again.

I was frustrated, I was angry, but more than anything, I was hurt. I didn't understand why that would be a problem. I couldn't ask my own mother for two dollars to buy lunch. And truth be told, two dollars wasn't enough to buy more than one item. I figured asking for the minimum would be less of a problem. I couldn't have been more wrong.

But, there was no time to feel sorry for myself. I had to figure something out and I had to do it quickly. The thought of not eating the whole school day scared me. I didn't know what I was going to do. I didn't even know where to start as far as creating a plan. So I decided to try to fight through the hunger pains. I lasted a couple more weeks without food, but it was really starting to affect the way my body felt during school.

I was too ashamed to ask anybody for help. So I sat there hungry, trying to fight through it. I remember being in class stressing over food. Wondering how or what I was going to eat every day. I tried my best to block it out of my mind, but my body was feeling worse by the hour. I started feeling light headed, losing energy in class. But still, I refused to say anything.

The feeling was worse during basketball season. I would have to practice on an empty stomach. It was a very scary feeling not knowing if I was going to pass out or not. Just imagine trying to run up and down a basketball court and practice on an intense level with no food or fuel in your system. After trying it a couple times, I realized my body could not withstand those conditions. I knew it was time to do something.

I had come up with a plan to steal a candy bar from lunch to satisfy my hunger. I had never stolen anything in my life, but it was the only thing I could think of. This became an everyday habit. My excuse was it was only a fifty-cent candy bar, and eating a candy bar was better than not eating anything.

Bad idea! It only made things worse. After about a month of the candy bar diet, I began to vomit on a daily basis. Sometimes I would get sick multiple times a day. At first I couldn't figure out what was going on with my body. It was a scary feeling.

My first thought was that I had a disease or something. It took me about two months, but I eventually figured out why I was getting sick. I noticed that every time I had eaten candy I would instantly throw it back up. And even though I was scared out of my mind, I refused to ask for help. I was embarrassed about my condition, and too ashamed to tell anyone what was going on. I figured it would be better if I dealt with it on my own.

I later found out that I had developed a disorder, called "cyclic vomiting syndrome." A person can develop this disorder through emotional distress, fasting, and eating certain foods like chocolate, with additives. I realized that I fit those descriptions very closely. I wasn't willingly fasting, but theoretically I was fasting. Plus, I was under a lot of stress.

But, God had other plans for me and my condition. I had vomited in the school hallway, three times one week because I wasn't able to make it to the bathroom fast enough. My teacher noticed what was going on and she intervened. Mrs. Sullivan my home room teacher was the first person to speak up about it.

One day after class, Mrs. Sullivan pulled me to the side and asked me what was going on. Still, I was reluctant to tell her the truth, but she knew I was keeping something from her. Me getting sick in the hallway made it obvious.

I decided to tell her what was going on since no one was around. I told Mrs. Sullivan about my situation and the real reason I was throwing up every day. Luckily for me, she felt pity for me and she offered to give me lunch money. Even though I desperately needed her help, I felt ashamed. I had grown up having to ask my friends parents for help. I was tired of doing that. I felt like I should've been able to ask my parents, not other people. I could only imagine how pathetic Mrs. Sullivan had thought I was. At the same time, I was very grateful for what she had done for me.

After about two weeks of feeling guilt for accepting Mrs. Sullivan's help, I was given an opportunity to work to earn money for lunch. I felt better working for it rather than asking someone to give me something. We made an agreement that I would wash chalk boards after school for Mrs. Sullivan and Mr. O'neill. On the days Mrs. Sullivan was not able to help me, Mr. O'neill allowed me to wash the chalk boards in his room for lunch money.

Initially, I felt embarrassed. I had a hard time asking for anything. However, through that experience I learned some valuable lessons. I learned that some people genuinely wanted to help me. And not only were they willing to help, but they were even willing to help without wanting anything in return. They also taught me how to work to earn things I needed in life.

I wasn't used to that. That really meant a lot to me. I will be forever grateful for Mrs. Sullivan and Mr. O'neill's help. I will never forget what they did for me. I'm not sure how they felt about it, but it was life changing for me. For someone to go out of their way to make sure I had food was a very big deal to me. Thank God for them.

CHAPTER 8

Back Where I Belong

MY JUNIOR SEASON turned out to be even better than my sophomore season at Catholic Central. I finished the season averaging twenty-four points per game, I led my team to a winning season, and I even had my first dunk of my career. I was named first team all-conference, all Clark County, and Special Mention All-Ohio.

But, even though I had just come off the most successful season of my basketball career, I wasn't happy playing at Catholic Central. I felt like my accomplishments were being discredited because I was playing for a small school. Plus, I had always dreamed of playing for Springfield South high school. That was where I really wanted to be.

My mom and coaches tried to convince me that Central would better prepare me for college, but my mind was set on playing for South. I was more than ready to play in Tiffany gymnasium (the name of Springfield South's gym). I was ready to play for Coach Ham. For years, I had dreamed of and putting on that blue and gold uniform. I had always wanted to play in front of the live crowds at the South games. Being a Wildcat was in my blood.

As kids, me and my friend Isiah Carson went to every home game at South. The South high basketball players were celebrities in our eyes. We knew who the best players were every season. I remember imitating their moves when we were at practice in the fifth grade. We waited for years to have our moment. And we finally got our chance during our senior year of high school. We were determined to make the best of it. We would go on to star on one of the best teams to ever play at South high.

My mother finally allowed me to transfer to South, after my coach at Central had left for another job. Coach Quincy left to coach the girls' basketball team at North high. For some reason, my mom trusted coach Quincy. And after he left my mom was okay with me transferring.

But, I didn't care either way. If him leaving allowed me to transfer to South, then so be it. I was finally going to be able to play for the Wildcats. I couldn't wait to get out there and play. The timing could not have been better. I had just come off my most successful season I had ever had on the basketball court. My confidence was at an all-time high. I was more than ready.

Ted Johnson, and His Deceitful Ways

But, before I transferred to South I experienced some controversy during AAU ball. Playing AAU was even more important than my season at Catholic Central. As I had gotten older I realized that the AAU teams were much better than they were when I was younger. The best players started teaming up to create super teams to compete for the nationals. The competition during the summer was over the top. Some teams would have five players from five different states in their starting line-ups. The gyms would be packed with people anxious to see the best of the best battle each other.

The summer going into my senior season, I had the best year of AAU I had ever experienced. I was playing for four different teams throughout the summer. I even had the luxury of traveling to big cities such as: Chicago, St. Paul, Minnesota, Louisville, and Lexington, Kentucky, and many other cities competing against some of the best players in the country. And even though I was playing against better competition, I was still able to score around twenty points per game throughout the summer. I even scored over thirty points in a couple games.

During the beginning of every fall, the sports writers ranked the top players in the state. Before the summer, I had only dreamed of being featured in the Prep Spotlight magazine. But, after having such a good season of AAU, I not only caught the attention of John Stovall, (editor of Prep Spotlight magazine) but I finished the summer ranked as the sixth best guard in the state of Ohio! Seeing my name in the magazine literally gave me butterflies. I just couldn't believe I had finally been ranked in the state.

After I had become ranked, the scouts were starting to come around. They were expecting me to have a great summer. My AAU team, Dayton Metro started off the summer in a very intense tournament. We played in Solon, Ohio in a tournament that featured teams from New York, Cleveland, Pennsylvania, and some of the best teams from Ohio.

The tournament also featured O.J. Mayo, one of the top players in the country. Mayo, was a seventh-grade kid who played varsity in Kentucky and averaged twenty points a game against high school players. He went on to play at the University of Southern California, and eventually made it to the NBA. The gym was filled with scouts because of Mayo being there.

I started the tournament coming off the bench, but finished as a starter after scoring the team high in our first game. I held onto that momentum and ended up winning the MVP of the Solon tournament. We won our first game in a blowout thirty-point win over a team from New York. But, we lost our second game to a team from Pennsylvania. It was a two-game elimination tournament, so we couldn't lose again. Otherwise we would be eliminated.

After the loss me and my teammates had to regroup. We made it tougher on ourselves by losing so early in the tournament. Now we were forced to get up early on Saturday morning, and fight our way back to the winner's bracket. That loss was the wake-up call I needed. I remember scoring over twenty-five points each game that Saturday morning. I was shooting so well that I was pulling up from the three-point line in fast break situations. To make it better I made a three pointer at the buzzer in the semi-finals when my team was down two, to win the game for us.

That shot put us back into the championship game. And we were set to face the team from Pennsylvania who had beaten us earlier in the tournament. I was excited about the opportunity to get revenge on those guys. Only this time the game meant more because the winner would take home the championship. I was more than ready for the rematch. My determination to win helped me come out strong, and score a game high thirty-two points. We won the championship, and I earned the tournament MVP!

After performing well in such a large tournament, I began to get calls from Division I college coaches. Eastern Michigan and Ohio University were the most consistent. Nothing made me happier than seeing the university's name come across the screen on the caller id. All the positive attention made me feel great. It was a great feeling to know that college coaches were interested in me playing for their schools.

That was literally a dream come true. But, even with the success I made sure to stay humble. I made sure to keep working to improve. Arrogance was not in my nature. I was determined to keep myself grounded and continue improving. I always felt like I could get better at some part of my game. Plus, there was no time to become complacent.

But as usual, good things were short lived in my life. After winning the MVP of the Solon tournament my coach (Ted Johnson) became envious of the attention I was receiving. I had played the same position as his son Charles Johnson, and we were on the same AAU team. My coach was more interested in looking out for his son than helping us win. And if sitting me gave his son a better chance of getting a scholarship, he was willing to do that.

When the college scouts wanted to get in touch with one of the players, they would contact the players AAU coach to get their information. So the coaches had to go through Ted Johnson before they could reach me. This is when his motive became obvious. After that tournament, my playing time decreased drastically. I barely played at all after the Solon tournament.

How does a player go from scoring over twenty-five points a game and willing his team to the championship, to not playing at all? In a matter of weeks, I went from MVP to a bench warmer. It just didn't make sense to me. There was no reasonable explanation for it.

Once the season was over I figured out what had happened. Not only did Ted Johnson take away my playing time, but he also bad mouthed me to the college scouts. I heard from another parent how Ted Johnson told the scouts that his son (Chris Johnson) was a better player than I was. That was disheartening considering I had known Ted Johnson since I was in the fifth grade. I had no idea he was capable of doing something like that.

Unfortunately for me his tactics paid off. Sitting me on the bench, talking down on me caused the coaches to lose interest in me. After the Solon tournament I never heard from those coaches again. I was crushed. I worked hard to make it to that level only to have my own coach take it away from me.

That happened to be yet another moment of severe disappointment. That situation sent me back into self-doubt. I went into depression trying to deal with that situation. Who knows what could've happened if my coach gave me the playing time I deserved?

Welcome to Wildcat Country!

Even though my summer of basketball ended horribly I did not have time to pout or complain. My senior season was only a few months away. And I was finally going to be playing for South, alongside my best friend Isiah Carson and Nate Miller. Those two were monsters on the court. I couldn't wait to get out there with them.

This was my chance to play for South. This was my chance to run out of the tunnel, with a South Wildcat jump suit on. This was my chance to play in Tiffany gymnasium. This was my chance to prove that I could play division one basketball. A chance to prove that I could perform at a high level against the big schools too. For years, I had dreamed of wearing that jump suit, running out onto Tiffany gymnasium and now I finally had a chance to.

Before the season had even started there was a lot of doubt about me contributing to the team. But, my experience playing at Catholic Central prepared me for what was to come. I already knew I would have people doubting me, waiting for me to fail. I had become accustomed to being judged. I grew up in Springfield, Ohio (voted the most miserable city in the United States)! So, people being negative didn't bother me as much as it used to.

Once the news spread that I was transferring, the local newspaper created an article that featured my situation. The article was written about me transferring from Catholic Central, a division four school, to Springfield South, a division one powerhouse. It was supposed to be positive, but of course it was turned into a negative story in my neighborhood.

Everywhere I went I heard the doubts and negative opinions from the local South fans. They told me that I couldn't make it at South. They said the transition would be too much for me. "Just because you are scoring thirty against the white boys, don't mean you can do that with the niggas! This is division one ball, not the county!" Those were the exact words I heard from numerous people in my neighborhood.

But, instead of letting it bother me, I used it as motivation. I had failed numerous times before by letting negative comments dictate my actions. This time I was focused on overcoming it. I was determined to show them, that not only could I play on the division one level, but I could contribute in a major way. I came into the season angry. I had something to prove. I was anxious to prove that I belonged at South and that my skills were good enough to play on that level.

Interacting with My Biological Father Again

Out of the blue, my biological father decided to move back to Springfield during my senior season. I had not seen or heard from my father since I left his house in Lansing, Michigan five years ago! Not a single word. And now he decides to come back when I am a senior in high school?

When I had first seen him I felt hatred for my father. Just seeing him brought back memories of what had happened when I was living with him in Lansing. It also brought back memories about my childhood, and not having a father present. Seeing him was bad enough, hearing him talk made me angrier.

I had been working, with a recruiting specialist for a program called, *college bound athletes*. The director put my videos on the internet in hopes scouts would see them. Apparently, my dad had seen the videos and decided to move back to Springfield to watch me play. My father even had the nerve to tell me that he had come back to watch me play, after seeing that I had gotten better. My fathers' exact words were, "I see you have gotten a lot better. I saw your videos on the internet, and I want to watch you play in your senior year." I couldn't believe he had the nerve to tell me that!

To add to my frustration, he attended all the home games that year. The simple fact that my father was in the stands bothered me. He was not present during all the years I was desperately in need of a father, but he comes when I am a senior in high school. But, even though I was bothered with my dad I could not allow it to distract me. I had to play through it. I had to stay focused on earning a college scholarship.

Whenever me and my dad interacted I kept the conversations short. I didn't express how I really felt, but deep down there was a lot I wanted to say to him. I was angry he left me. I was angry I found out he was my father when I was thirteen years old. I was angry that I went to live with him and his girlfriend did those things to me. I had not forgiven my father for those things. I was even more angry that he never expressed remorse about what had happened. In his mind, it wasn't a big deal.

So my frustration lingered on for years. I felt abandoned by him and now he just comes back like everything is okay? I wanted him to feel what I felt. So when it came time for me and the other seniors to walk out for senior night, I made it clear that my father was not to walk out with me. I had not seen or talked to my father in five years! I wasn't going to let him just come back in the picture and pick up like nothing happened. There was no way I was going to let him do that. Plus, no one knew who my father was. I didn't want to deal with everyone asking questions about who the strange man was walking out there with me.

Despite all the negative peoples' opinions, and my father coming back to Springfield, the season started off great. I was determined to have a great season regardless. I had waited a very long time to play for South. I wasn't going to let anyone ruin that. Just having the chance to wear the Wildcat uniform was special to me.

Our first official game was against Tecumseh. They were a division one school, but they weren't very good. We were expected to beat them badly and we did. We ended up winning by fifty points on their home floor. I finished my first official game as a Wildcat with seventeen points. However, our next game would be our first real test. We played Troy in our first home game of the season. Troy featured a post player who was 6'9, and two tough guards.

To everyone's surprise, Troy beat us on our home floor! A lack of leadership and team chemistry cost us that game. To make things worse, Nate and I nearly got into a fight during the game. That loss caused an uproar in the city. The expectations were very high and for us to lose in the second game of the season was a shock to everyone! Nobody expected us to lose that game. We weren't expected to lose any games.

The players, parents, and fans were stunned about the early loss. It was so bad that an angry fan waited outside of our locker room, and tried to fight our coach. Tensions were high and tempers were flaring. The fans were looking for someone to blame, so they used our coach as the scapegoat.

But when I look back I realize that loss early in the season helped us. We needed that. It was the wake-up call that made us work harder. It also forced us to put our differences aside to work toward our goal. Win a state title. After that loss we went on to win twelve games in a row, in route to one the best seasons in Springfield South history.

Individually, I finished the season averaging nineteen points per game, while shooting fifty percent from the three-point range. Nate, and Isiah both averaged seventeen points each. Then we had Jabril, who scored around twelve points per game, plus Von Davis scoring about eight points per game.

As a team we averaged 78.2 points per game in just 32 minutes of game time. We went 23-3 that season (two losses coming to the eventual state champion, Hamilton), our other loss came to Troy who finished the season as the second ranked team in the state. We beat seven teams who were ranked top ten in the state at some point in the season. And in the tournament, we advanced to the regional finals.

Things weren't so bad off the court at that time. My home life was chaotic, but my family had food on the table and all the utilities were up to date. It was never a normal home, but things were going better than usual. For once I felt a sense of contentment with life. Well at least for the moment.

To make things even better, I had just met my first serious girlfriend. We were inseparable throughout our entire relationship. That was until Angel's mother figured out how serious we were. Her mother had a problem with my living conditions. She didn't like the fact that my family was poor. She felt I was not good enough to date her daughter.

It was the first time either of us had been in a relationship and we really thought we were in love. But we were just young kids. In reality we didn't have a clue of what love was. We liked each other a lot though. We would talk on the phone for hours and spend every moment together. But like every good situation, there comes bad moments. The longer we were together the more her mother tried to separate us.

To add to the tension, I was a senior and she was a junior in high school. We knew there would be a time when I had to leave her to go to school. Despite the move we agreed to stay together, but her mother was not going to let that happen. Her mother was determined to move her away so that we could not keep in contact with each other. My girlfriend responded by lying to me about her taking her birth control. She had been on it since I had known her, but she stopped taking it and never told me about it. Needless to say she ended up pregnant.

The pregnancy was confirmed after I had left for school. Initially we both panicked, but the damage was already done. We both knew we were way too young to be raising a kid. But after praying and thinking about the situation, I accepted the responsibility. I figured we should keep the baby. But Angel was afraid of what her mother would do. Those factors made her reluctant to keep the baby. After months of arguing she decided to get the abortion despite me being against it.

It crushed me to find out that she went and got the procedure done. She waited until she was five months pregnant to do it! The thought of killing a baby really got under my skin. It brought that dreaded feeling back of feeling hopeless. I couldn't believe what she had just told me. I couldn't believe she went and got the abortion even though I had told her not to. She had even asked me for half of the money for it, but I refused to send it. I did not want her to go through with it.

I secretly battled depression after that situation. It took me four years to completely get over it. I couldn't get that image of an innocent baby being killed, out of my head. I couldn't forgive Angel for what she had done. Especially considering I told her not to go through with it. I knew I would never feel the same about her after that. So I broke off our relationship. And like every other major problem in my life I kept it to myself. I was too embarrassed to share it with anyone. Telling anyone about my personal problems was never an option. In my mind, people would look at me funny or judge me once they found out the way I was living. I've only told one other person about the abortion situation for that reason.

CHAPTER 9

Coming into My Own

AFTER THE INCIDENT with Ted Johnson the college coaches stopped calling. I had gone from hopes of playing division one college basketball to not knowing if I would play college ball at all. The letters and the phone calls from the big schools had stopped coming in altogether. It destroyed my confidence.

To make things worse, I had no other plans for my life besides going to college. Basketball was my best chance of getting into college. If I didn't go to school, I didn't know what I was going to do with my life. I was so determined to go to college and play basketball that I had never imagined doing anything else. Just the thought of not playing basketball was enough to drive me crazy.

Luckily for me, one coach had continued to send letters throughout the whole process, coach Steve Moore from the college of Wooster. I had played in their high school shootout the summer of my sophomore year, at Catholic Central. Luckily, I caught the attention of the coaches at Wooster. I remember going to the Wooster shootout with only six players. Three of those players had no varsity experience at all.

During the College of Wooster shootout, I was fortunate to have one of the best shooting performances of my career. I knew I had to play on an elite level if my team was going to win. Otherwise we would lose and be sent home. The timing of the shooting performance could not have been better. It seemed like every shot I put up went in.

In my mind, I was going to score every time I got the ball. We ended up winning the shootout with just six players. My determination to win caught the eyes of the coaches at the College of Wooster. After that performance they began to recruit me to join their team. From there we ended up staying in contact throughout my senior season.

I still had hope that the bigger schools would come back around, but they didn't. It didn't help that my frame was not built for college basketball. My size, along with the Ted Johnson incidents hurt my chances of playing division one college ball. I even had a coach tell me that I was skilled enough to play division one basketball, but my size was an issue. I was 6 feet tall, but I only weighed 147 pounds! My body was nowhere near ready for the next level.

So I ended up committing to play basketball at the College of Wooster around May 2004. I was grateful to be going to college, but still disappointed about not going to a division one school. I remember telling my high school coach that I didn't want my commitment to be published in the paper because I was ashamed.

As kids all we ever talked about was playing for a division one school. I did not reach my goal and it bothered me. But I had to look at the big picture and be grateful to be playing college ball at all. I told myself that I would work hard make the best of the opportunity and finish college no matter what.

In the summer going into my freshman year at Wooster, I went to work the team basketball camp. While working the camp I got a chance to play against some of the other recruits who were coming to the college. I also played against a few of the upperclassmen there who were still on the team. During the day myself and the other incoming freshmen helped run the camp by coaching the kids and demonstrating drills.

At night when the campers were in their dorm rooms we scrimmaged in the upstairs gym. This would be my first time playing against my teammates. It was also the first time Coach Moore would see me play against college guards. So this was much more than just an ordinary open gym. In my mind, it was more of a test to see how well I would perform.

The pressure of playing in front of coach Moore became even more intense after finding out I was the top recruit in the class of 2008. Rodney

Mitchell, one of the best guards to play at the College of Wooster, informed me of the top recruit status. He told me the older guys were probably going to come after me, to see if I could handle the physicality of college basketball.

Before Rodney told me I had no idea that coaches ranked their recruits. I was even more shocked to find out that I was the top recruit. However, there were good and bad things about being in that position. It felt great to be recognized, but it also brought more pressure. I knew everyone would be expecting a lot from me.

Even though I was nervous, I tried to focus on one game at a time. My plan was to adjust to the college game and continue to improve. Once we started playing, I noticed that college ball players were much more physical and much faster than high school players. After that first game I knew that I had work to do. I had to get stronger and I had to get quicker immediately.

My team won four games in a row, but I did not perform on the level I would've liked to. I was disappointed in myself. I missed a lot of shots that I normally make. I didn't score the way I would have liked to. I just didn't feel like myself. I knew I had to redeem myself once I was given the chance.

It was strange though. Everyone else thought I played well. I was praised for playing well against the other guards. I appreciated their compliments, but my mind was set on being much better than what I had showed. My performance nothing to be proud of.

After the camp, I had gone back home to Springfield. I had stayed home for two months before it was time to report back to Wooster for school. As soon as I arrived back to Springfield all the drama hit me at once. It was a bunch of chaos at my house as usual. My younger sisters were now in middle school and were really acting out. Sneaking boys in the house, talking back, arguing with mom.

None of our fathers were around so I had to deal with it and it drove me crazy. But those weren't the only issues I faced in my household. I had been saving money to buy books for school after working my first job for Ansley's painting crew. I hid the money in my room because I didn't have a bank account at that time. Someone in my family went in my room and stole the money I was saving.

I was so angry that I went off on everyone in the house. It was situations like that, that motivated me to want to get away. I imagine most freshman being worried about leaving home. Going away to live in an unfamiliar place had to be difficult. I'm sure it was intimidating. But I was just the opposite. I couldn't wait to get away from Springfield. I knew college would bring challenges, but it had to be a better than living with my family.

A Surreal Moment!

It was August of 2004, my first semester as a college student! I couldn't believe that I was actually in college! I couldn't believe that I was going to be playing college basketball! I did it! My dream was now a reality! All those years of practicing. All those years of dreaming about it and now it was actually happening. Everything seemed surreal to me. I didn't know what to think or what to expect. But I was extremely excited about the opportunity. There was so much to learn! So many experiences to indulge in. So many memories to create!

No one in my family had ever gone to college. That was a major accomplishment in itself. I was going to be the first to do it. The only bad thing was I couldn't ask anyone for advice. Both my parents had dropped out of high school. So I had to figure things out on my own. But it didn't matter. I was going to find a way to get through it.

To be honest, I was excited about the opportunity, but I had no idea of how I was going to pull it off. I was so naive to the college experience that I didn't even know what questions to ask on my visit. In fact, I don't remember asking any questions at all. I was just happy to be there. Happy to be away from Springfield. Now I just had to find a way to finish school. Going back home was not an option.

Luckily for me, I had two great men in my corner. Coach Moore and Rodney Mitchell. They helped me in numerous ways. They brought things to my attention that I never would have thought of. I had no idea of where to start the process of living on a college campus. How to schedule classes or anything. They made the whole process manageable. I'm still thankful for everything they had done for me.

Rodney Mitchell was one of the nicest people I had ever met. Rodney had graduated from the College of Wooster in 2004. He came from a similar background and played ball at the college. With his experience, he was able to help me adjust to the small town of Wooster. He gave me tips and advice about school and how he adapted to living in Wooster. He told me what to expect, he told me what practice was going to be like, he even told me where I could get a haircut, and what professors were his favorites. All of his advice helped my confidence. Talking with Rodney made me feel like I had a chance of graduating. I can't thank him enough for what he did.

Coach Moore also went above and beyond to help me out. He answered every question I had. He even helped me advise a plan to get through the initial process of registering for classes, finding the buildings, and he even helped me choose my major. Coach even took time out of his busy schedule to show me where my classes were. I really appreciate everything he and Rodney had done to help me. It's something I will never forget.

Trouble in the Classroom

After getting advice from Rodney and Coach Moore it was time to start school. Even though classes had officially started, I was still in the process of taking everything in. I was still in shock. The whole environment in Wooster was completely different than what I was used to. I felt like I was on another planet. Everyone was nice. Everyone was always smiling. The people in Wooster were very friendly. No one gave me dirty looks or had negative comments.

I rarely ever heard ambulance sirens going off. I didn't see police riding up and down the street. The biggest shocker for me was people actually wanted to help me. They wanted to see me succeed. That was one of the biggest surprises of the whole experience. The atmosphere was completely the opposite of what I had seen in Springfield.

Initially, I felt like they were playing a joke on me. They seemed way too enthusiastic about helping. My teachers, my advisers, my coaches, and even my teammates were very supportive. It was something I had never experienced. In my hometown people were much more likely to talk bad about me than they were to help. It seemed like no one wanted to see you succeed. It wasn't like that in Wooster. I loved it though. I loved the fact that I could relax for the first time in my life. The simple fact of knowing people around me wanted to see me succeed made me feel better about myself.

College life started off great, but with everything in life there are positive and negative things that come with it. I wasn't expecting to come to college and breeze through. There was so much I had to learn. I figured there would be tough times, but there were a couple things that caught me off guard.

The first thing was how serious my professors were about missing class. I figured that in the large classrooms the professors wouldn't notice if I came to class or not. I could not have been more wrong! I had adopted this mentality at South high, but I had to snap out of it quickly.

At South I could skip class, not study, take the test, and still get a least a "B". That wasn't the case at Wooster. I was ignorant to that type of environment, but they gave me a quick dose of reality. I was placed on academic probation during my first semester of school. Coach Moore was furious! He called me into his office and went berserk after finding out how many classes I had missed. And to be honest I couldn't blame him.

I had missed over twenty classes in my first semester of school! I don't know what I was thinking, but I knew I had to fix it. Otherwise I would be sent back to Springfield with no plan for my life. So I met with the instructor of the probation program, completed the requirements, and was off probation in four weeks! From that point on I didn't miss more than five classes per semester and I kept my grade point average at a "B". I put myself in a situation where I had to prove that I belonged in school. At the same time, I needed that to keep me focused.

The other negative aspects were unintentional, but really hurt my confidence. In one of my sociology classes, we were covering the subject of "poverty" and how it affected people daily. I had never even heard the word "poverty" before that class. I didn't have a clue of what they were talking about. But once my professor broke down the meaning of poverty, what it looked like, and how people in poverty lived, I knew exactly what he was talking about.

After hearing the professor describe the characteristics of poverty I had just realized that I had been living in poverty my entire life! To make it even more embarrassing I had become accustomed to it. I was so naive that I thought it was how everyone lived.

It cut deep when my professor read the statistics, of the percentage of people who graduate college coming from rough neighborhoods. He pretty much said, that if a person grew up in a neighborhood surrounded by poverty that they will not amount to anything. Those people would most likely turn out to be low life criminals, who would end up in prison or dead at an early age.

One statistic bothered me even more others though. When my professor read off the percentage of people who graduate college if their parents did not graduate high school. That statistic bothered me the most. I learned that less than two percent of people whose parents dropped out of high school graduate from college.

Hearing that statistic made me feel like college wasn't for me. Once I had heard that I felt like I didn't have a chance of graduating. I honestly thought about sneaking out of the classroom and never going back. I thought to myself "if both my parents dropped out of high school, I have no chance of graduating college. The statistics my professor just read confirmed it."

But I couldn't allow myself to give up. After about an hour of contemplating quitting school, I gathered myself and created a plan. I made a decision that day that I was going to graduate college no matter what. I was going to study and take my education as serious as I took basketball. The preparation had to be equal in both areas. I didn't feel confident, and I didn't know how I was going to do it, but I was going to find a way.

Earning a Spot

I guess you can say the troubles I was having in the classroom were expected. But what took me by surprise were the troubles I faced on the basketball court. I had been used to having my way, scoring so easily in high school. I just knew that if nothing else I could make an impact through my offensive skills. But I quickly realized that things were much more difficult on the collegiate level.

The game was so much faster. Everyone was so much stronger. It didn't help that I only weighed 147 pounds. At that time, my max on the bench press was a laughable 140 pounds, which was the second weakest on the team (the guy with the weakest bench press, quit the team before our first practice). I was literally being tossed around in practice. Every contact drill was a challenge for me.

Once I realized how weak I was, I knew I had to rely on my speed and quickness to be effective. I was wrong about that too. The older players would just hand check and use their strength on defense to stop me. And coach didn't call many fouls in practice, so there was no way I could be effective.

After struggling on the court because of my lack of strength, I started working out five days a week. I had to catch up with the other guards on the team. On top of lifting I was doing three hundred push-ups every night. I was determined to get stronger and I was determined to get stronger quickly.

By the spring of my freshman season I increased my bench press to 185 pounds. That helped in many ways. I could instantly feel the difference on the court. I could fight through screens more effectively, and I was able to drive past defenders who used their hands on defense. Getting stronger changed my entire game.

I finished my freshman season as the third leading scorer on the team at ten points per game. I also shot above fifty percent from the field, which put me in the top ten of the conference in shooting percentage. That was good, but I still felt like I had work to do. I felt like I was a better player than what I had showed during my freshman season.

I was very inconsistent during my freshman season. I had to continue to get stronger. Plus, I had a lot to learn on the defensive end. On a positive note, I scored the second most points by a freshman in school history, in a national tournament game against Baldwin Wallace. In that game I scored twenty-seven points, recorded five assists, and four rebounds to help us beat a very good team. That was the confidence boost I needed going into my sophomore season.

Separating Myself from the Pack

The summer before my sophomore season, would be one of the most challenging summers I would experience, while attending Wooster. First, I had to go back to Springfield once the school year was over. When I arrived home I noticed that nothing had changed. There was drama at home, drama in the neighborhood, and everyone was still doing the same things. But it felt even worse than before because I had gotten away from all the negativity. I had become accustomed to living peacefully in Wooster. I didn't want to deal with the drama anymore. Just being back in that environment made me feel depressed.

In Wooster, I was able to relax in my dorm room without any drama. And for the first time in my life I felt comfortable. I could take time to think. I finally had a piece of mind. I wasn't living my life stressed out. I wasn't expecting problems every day.

But as soon as I arrived in Springfield I was reminded of why I was so desperate to get out of there. There was non-stop drama every day at home. I couldn't find a summer job, there was nowhere to play ball, and nowhere to lift without paying an expensive gym membership (which I could not afford). I hated being back home. I immediately started counting down the days until it was time to return back to school. A peaceful place where I could breathe, I could relax, focus only on school, and basketball.

Once I had arrived back in Wooster I didn't waste any time getting back into my routine. Not only was I lifting weights, but I was watching film from the previous season. I was determined to learn from last season's mistakes. I remember being angry with myself on what I thought were "weak performances" during the games of my freshman season. I became frustrated watching myself play and not make an impact on the game. I told myself that I was going to be more aggressive during my sophomore season.

I would soon be on a path to destroy every opponent I faced. I worked on rebuilding my game. I made sure to do it quietly though. There was no need to talk about my plans. I would let my performance do the talking. I wanted my coaches, and teammates to see the difference opposed to me talking about it. Boasting didn't suit me or what I stood for.

COMING INTO MY OWN

Coach Bud Board

Playing against Bud Board and the Wittenberg Tigers added to my motivation to want to be better. Bud Board was the most unprofessional coach I had ever played against. There were no boundaries with him. Coaches and athletes sometimes say and do things we normally wouldn't say in the midst of competition. And in big games people tend to get caught up in the moment. But there are some things that should not happen as professionals, especially the head coach of the team. He would even tell false stories to local reporters to keep drama started. Especially after we had beaten them.

I first noticed how petty Bud Board was after he refused to shake my hand. We were going through the line after we had beaten Wittenberg during my freshman season and he walked right past me. He wouldn't even look in my direction to shake my hand. My initial reaction was shock. I couldn't believe the head coach of the team would not shake my hand. As a player, it was drilled in my head to play the game with integrity. So to see the head coach of a college team do something like that, surprised me.

But after pondering over the situation I started to become angry. That anger turned into motivation. Motivation to play better. Motivation to do whatever it took to beat Wittenberg. I was determined to take it out on his team. My plan was to make his players suffer for his unprofessional-ism. That was going to be my pay back to him refusing to shake my hand.

Bud Board would not stop there though. The day before our game during my freshman season, he told the local paper in Springfield that I only went to Wooster because my grades were not good enough for Wittenberg. He also said that he recruited me only to draw me away from Wooster. Meaning he was not interested in me as a basketball player. He just did not want his rival to pick me up.

After Bud Boards comments in the paper, the Wittenberg fans really began to show hatred towards me. He had given them extra negative energy to use against me. It was already an intense rivalry between Wittenberg and Wooster. Me being from Springfield (Wittenberg is in Springfield) only made it worse. Having a guy from Springfield to root against gave them more ammunition to hate Wooster.

The Wittenberg fans would arrive to the gym hours before the game was scheduled to start just to taunt me. The game wouldn't start until eight that night, but they would arrive at noon just to try to frustrate me. And they were willing to say just about anything to get me off my game.

However, they failed to realize that I had already been through hell on, and off the court. I had been talked about by my own family and people in my neighborhood. I had already been criticized in local papers and on the internet. At that point I was used to being talked about in a negative way. I was used to dealing with criticism from opponents and critics. And through experience I learned to use that negative energy as motivation to succeed. When my opponents taunted me or disrespected me I played better. In my mind, I was going to give them more reasons to root against me. I was going to shoot better, run faster, jump a little higher, be a step quicker, and most importantly find a way to help my team win the game.

CHAPTER 10

A New Level

THE FIRST VISUAL sign of improvement came during team testing day in the fall. Testing day consisted of the team meeting in the weight room to see how much we could lift on bench press and leg press. During my freshman season I could only lift six plates on the leg press while the rest of the team used seven plates. And I maxed out at a pathetic 140 pounds on the bench press.

This time I was able to lift seven plates on each leg for twenty-one reps! I then maxed out at 185 pounds on the bench press! I surprised everyone in the weight room that day. I had increased my leg press by seventy pounds and I had increased my bench press by forty-five pounds. I could see the excitement on my coach's face, as he flashed a wide grin after I completed the testing.

Once we stepped on the court it was time to really show how hard I had worked to get better. I was two steps quicker and forty-five pounds stronger than I was the previous season. And it really showed in my game. My teammates could no longer stop me by hand checking. I used new found strength and speed to move through it.

I performed well in practice. I performed well during our scrimmage games. But I knew the real test would come during the season. In my mind the improvements only mattered if I performed well when the games really counted. If I didn't show improvements during the season, all my hard work meant nothing.

I felt decent though. My confidence levels had risen after working so hard in the off-season. I anxiously waited for the first game of the season. I was ready to prove that I was a better player than what I showed during my freshman season. Even though I felt like I was ready, I never could have predicted the season I was going to have that year.

My goal on the court and my goal in life is to learn from mistakes, and continue to improve. I did that by facing my flaws head on then working hard to overcome them. My problem was that I over-criticized myself. Me being too hard on myself caused me to lose hope at times. There were rarely any times where I thought things would work out for the better. However, that season would be just the opposite.

I also took some pressure off myself by setting realistic goals. I wasn't the type of player to tell myself I had to score a certain amount of points to be successful. I did not look at the records or the record books. My only goal was to continue to improve. Improve each game, continue to learn, and perform on an elite level consistently. To do whatever it took to help my team win. That was the ultimate goal. Win!

I was fortunate to have the gift of being able to score in a variety of ways. I took pride in frustrating my opponent's coaches and the defenders guarding me. I was able to make an impact by working on specific skills to make my game more complex. To make my game unpredictable.

I made sure I was able to score going either left or right. I put in work to ensure I could shoot at an efficient level, on a consistent basis. I put in hours of work perfecting my three point shot, the mid-range shot, and even worked on getting to the rim. I also made it a habit to take quality shots without forcing them.

Those factors really helped me that season. Those attributes allowed me to lead my team to the conference title. I also led the conference in scoring, while shooting fifty-five percent from the field, and forty-seven percent from the three-point line. Those percentages landed me in the top ten in both categories in our conference. To add to those statistics, I made the biggest shot of my career to beat our rival Wittenberg.

The Biggest Shot of My Career!

We were playing Wittenberg on our home court. We were ranked second in the nation, they were ranked fifth in the nation. The gym was packed to capacity, full of screaming, yelling, excited fans. Nearly four thousand people anxious to see the outcome. It was the type of game I had dreamed of playing in as a kid. I had never played in front of a crowd like that before that game.

To make it more exciting we were tied for first place in the conference for the second year in a row. So the winner of that game would claim the title. All those factors were important, but the main thought in my mind was the beating they had given us during my freshman season. We were the number one ranked team in the nation. And a victory against Wittenberg would've given Coach Moore his 500th win. To make it more special we were playing on our home floor.

Wittenberg came into our gym and destroyed the whole ceremony by beating us by eighteen points! They had completely taken the excitement out of the gym. We even canceled the celebration for Coach Moore. That loss destroyed our team's morale.

It felt worse to hear them celebrating in the locker room beside us. That loss was embarrassing to say the least! I was so frustrated that I went to the gym the next morning to shoot around. I felt like I had to be better for the next game. I could not believe how bad they had beaten us. I took that loss personally. I took it upon myself to make a difference the next time we faced them. There was no way I could let my team lose like that again.

Which is why the game in my sophomore season was much more than a rival game. This was our chance to get revenge. Plus, it was a chance for us to win the conference title outright. Both teams were prepared to scrap until the last play. Both fan sections were prepared to make the gym as loud as possible.

You could feel the hatred between both teams in the air. Practice was much more intense throughout the week. Our locker room was filled with negative quotes that Wittenberg players said about us. Alumni from both teams fought over tickets to be able to see this game. Our coaches even took jabs at each other throughout the week leading up to the game.

I remember standing, waiting on jump ball, and being amazed at how rowdy the crowd was. I was so hyped up on adrenaline, that I could bounce off the wall and not feel the pain. I wanted to win so badly. I wasn't the only one who felt that way though. Both teams were amped up ready to do whatever it took to win.

We had battled furiously throughout the first thirty-nine minutes of the game. Both teams were bruised and battered from fighting so hard. We battled for every loose ball. We fought for every rebound. Every shot was contested. The fouls were harder than usual. You could sense the fans were growing tired from screaming, but still they refused to slow down. The coaches were even sweating from yelling, and pacing back and forth on the sidelines.

By the end of the second half both teams were playing on adrenaline. The game was going to be decided in the last minute. I was extremely tired myself, but I refused to show any signs of weakness. I could not let my team lose. I constantly reminded myself to fight through the fatigue.

I thought about them beating us twice my freshman year. I thought about all the shots I missed, and how I let my team down in those losses. I thought about the Wittenberg players running through our gym celebrating their victory on our home court. And I blacked out.

The game was tied with about thirty seconds left. I got the ball on a side out of bounds play, drove to the right wing, and made a short jumper to put us up by two. Our fans roared with excitement after the bucket. They got the ball, passed it to their best player, Dan Russ and scored right away, tying the game up with ten seconds left on the clock. Now their fans are going crazy as the momentum seems to be on their side. Instead of calling timeout coach let me bring the ball up the court.

I walked the ball up the court as both cheering sections roared with nervous, excitement. The ball is in my hands and I know the whole gym is watching me. All I'm thinking about is scoring to give us the victory. There is no way I am going to miss. I just can't.

As I dribble up the court, Tom walks up to set a screen. I waved him off so that I have more room to get away from the defenders. I knew that if I had dribbled anywhere near the post player, they would trap me at the top of the key. But if I went one on one it would be much easier to score.

Now it's just me and my opponent, one on one at the top of the key.

The rest of my teammates were standing near the baseline, waiting on me to make a move. Coach did not call a play. He was leaving the game in my hands. Everybody in the gym is watching the ball. I glance at the clock, and its winding down below ten seconds. My plan was to wait until there were seven seconds left to make my move. Then attack an open area on the court to get a shot off.

My first thought was to drive to the rim. So I start to dribble toward the defender to see how he reacts. He starts to back off, but the help side defense is waiting for me to drive. I also notice one of his teammates to my left, starting to come up to help. I knew he was coming to trap me and if I waited too long I would put myself in a bad position. All of the sudden, the help side defender starts sprinting toward me to force me to pass the ball. At that point I knew I had to get a shot off quickly. So, I take an aggressive dribble toward the initial defender to force him to back off. As he backs off, he gives me just enough space to get a shot off. After I make the move I release the ball from about twenty-nine feet from the rim with about six seconds left on the clock.

As soon as I release the ball the entire gym goes silent. There's almost four thousand people in the gym, and they're all watching the ball in the air. Anxious to see the result. Everyone's eyes are wide open. It seemed like the ball was in the air for ten minutes.

I felt confident about the shot though. I took a shot that I knew I could make. I felt good as the ball left my hands. And before I can blink again it goes through the net! The Wooster crowd roared so loudly I thought my ears were going to bleed!

Everyone is jumping around, going crazy, in awe of the shot!!! I even showed a rare sign of celebration, as I ran to half court and jumped as high as I could pumping my fist in the air. As soon as I landed Wittenberg called timeout. My teammates, then ran onto the court with excitement, hugging me, and yelling as the crowd is going crazy in the background!

The shot puts us up by three points with just four seconds left on the clock. After the timeout, Wittenberg takes the ball out of bounds, forces a quick shot, and misses! As soon as the buzzer sounds the Wooster fans storm the court. It was pandemonium to say the least! They picked me up on their shoulders, and carried me through the gym! It was a scene I will never forget. There is nothing like making a shot to beat your hometown rival, on your home floor. The feeling was indescribable!

The city of Wooster was ecstatic after that game. There were parties going on all over campus, until five the next morning! Everywhere I went people were coming up to me, hugging me, talking about the shot. It was a humbling experience to bring so much excitement and happiness to our school.

I woke up the next morning to get a newspaper and there it was! A picture of the students holding me up on their shoulders. That same picture was all over the website, the school paper, local paper and even the Springfield newspaper. To add to the article, a local car dealership even advertised their commercial by using the clip from my shot against Wittenberg. That was definitely something I had never experienced. I could not believe I was being featured in a local television commercial.

Finishing Them Off

The first match-up with Wittenberg was very intense to say the least. We had played our rival in a sold-out gym on our home floor, for the lead in our conference race. To make it even more intense, the game ended on a three point shot that lead to pandemonium. Believe it or not the second game would be even more intense than the first one.

Both Wittenberg, and our team had gone undefeated since our match-up and now we were ranked as the number one and number two teams in the nation! We were considered the best two teams in all of division III basketball! It was the first time that the top two teams had ever played each other during the season. The anticipation could not have been any higher than what it was.

I remember that being the toughest week of practice I have ever experienced as a basketball player. We had film session three times that week. We practiced an hour longer every day of the week. And instead of our normal routine, we practiced specifically for Wittenberg. Every drill was designed to help us counter their tactics for the big game.

Everyone on campus was talking about the game. Professors, students, even campus staff were anxiously waiting for the game. Each player was given four tickets for our families, but even that wasn't enough. Our family members were plotting on ways to get extra tickets to see the big game. We knew in advance that the rematch was going to be one of the biggest games we had ever played in.

After a week of preparation, it was finally game day. Today would be Wittenberg's chance to get revenge for us beating them earlier in the year. On the other hand, it was also an opportunity for us to clinch the conference title. All the trash talking was irrelevant at that point. It was time to play.

Another Distraction

To add to the drama, I had trouble off the court with my family. I received a call from the Springfield News-Sun, every year before the Wittenberg game to conduct an interview. The reporters did a story on me being from Springfield and playing for Wooster (Wittenberg's rival). But for some reason I was asked to conduct two interviews this year. At first I did not pay any attention to it. I completed the interview and went on about my day.

But when I arrived to my house on game day, I was blind-sided by drama that came from the second interview. I thought back to the second interview and noticed that the reporter asked a few questions about my high school coach at Catholic Central. But again I did not think anything of it.

Well, apparently my coaches' wife had called the local newspaper and told them how much coach Quincy had done for me. Claiming he had gotten me into school and he was the reason I had reached success on the basketball court. To make it worse, the reporter left out other people who had influenced me along the way. The article only spoke of coach Quincy, claiming he had done everything for me.

That article offended my mom because she felt she should've been mentioned. And when I walked into the door the day of the game, my younger sisters confronted me and asked me why I left my mom out of the article. They expressed to me that my mom's feelings were hurt because of it. I instantly became frustrated, because I had no idea that they were going to print the article, and make it seem like coach Quincy was the main reason I was playing college ball. I was even more annoyed at the fact that my family decided to bring that up, the day I was going to play in the biggest game of my career. But instead of arguing I just left the house, and went back to the hotel with the rest of my team. I didn't have time to deal with that. My mind had to be in the right place in order to be able to function in an important game like that.

Back to Business

After getting back to the hotel we had a short film session in coaches' room. From there we went to Wittenberg to have a live walk through on their home court. We arrived at the gym around 1:00 pm, and we were set to play at 8:30 that night. Believe it or not, there were Wittenberg fans waiting for me when we arrived for the walk through. One of them continued to walk up and down the hallway, saying things trying to frustrate me. He made negative comments about me trying to get a reaction. Little did he know it was only giving me more ammunition to play better that night.

After the walk through, we went back to the hotel to get some rest. While sitting in the room, watching television, everyone's phones began going off. Friends and fellow students were calling to tell us about the fight that had taken place between the students in front of the gym.

Apparently, Wooster students, and Wittenberg's students had gotten into a scuffle while waiting to buy tickets. This only added more fuel to the fire. We then found out that the game had sold out that afternoon, making it the first sellout in over twenty years at the Wittenberg gym!

A couple hours pass and it is finally game time. We arrive to the gym, and as expected it is pure chaos. The lobby is full of people, the gym is packed to capacity, and it is very loud. You can feel the energy in the air as we walk through the crowd to get to our locker room.

Again, I'm greeted with boo's and chants from Wittenberg fans as I head to the locker room. This time a different fan of Wittenberg's started walking past our locker room trying to antagonize me. Part of me wanted to confront him, but I knew it would only feed into his plan. So I sat in the locker room quietly. Angry, anxious to play. I knew in my mind that I was going to come out and set the tone for us to win. That

Wittenberg fan was going to pay for every word he said.

Its finally time for the game to start. By this time, I am so worked up that I can't sit still. I couldn't wait to unleash my frustration out on the Wittenberg players. The annoying Wittenberg fans had given me all the motivation I had needed to play with fierce energy. Plus, I had support from my family during this game. It was a great feeling to see them, along with my middle school coach in the stands. I had my mom, my sisters, my aunt Margy, Coach Park, and my little brother watching. That was extra motivation to perform well that night.

It is game time! Both student sections are standing up waving towels as we stand at center court for the jump ball. And as usual, I am in a different mode. All I'm thinking about is playing ferociously, scoring in every way possible. My goal was to completely take over the game. I was determined to silence the Wittenberg fans for good!

The game started as it normally did. Both teams came out swinging for the fence. But this time we dominated the entire game. We lead from jump ball until the final buzzer, never falling behind. It was a great team effort overall.

Individually, I started the game strong, and I held onto that momentum to lead us to the victory. I finished with a game high twenty-four points, I shot 9-12 from the field, added five assists, and four rebounds. That win helped us clinch the conference championship meaning we would host the tournament for the second year in a row.

That was a wonderful feeling. First, making the game winning shot at our gym. Then performing well to help us win the second game to clinch the conference title. We had beaten our bitter rival in both meetings that year. It seemed like that shot symbolized how my sophomore season would go.

The awards just kept piling up. I never would've thought I would be named player of the year in our conference. I was honored, and surprised at the same time. Yet, there would be another surprise, that felt even better than being named MVP of our conference. I made the All-Region and All-American teams that season!

Before that season I had only dreamed of becoming an All-American. I never thought I would actually be placed on an All-American team. I also became the first player in the College of Wooster basketball history, to lead the league in scoring, and be named the league player of the year as a sophomore.

I had become used to the attention that came with being a high school star, but college was much more intense. In college, we had the campus newspaper, the local newspaper, the school website, and our games were displayed on local television. People in the city were going to see your face, and hear your name if you were successful.

After that season I was known around the city of Wooster. Everywhere I went people approached me, and gave me praise for my basketball skills. Both kids and adults began asking for my autograph. I could not believe what was taking place. There was so much positive energy in Wooster. Still, the biggest surprise was the television commercial that featured me making the shot to beat Wittenberg! I couldn't believe what I was seeing on the television, when it came on.

I was extremely grateful for all the positive attention I had received, but I wasn't satisfied. I still had more to accomplish. The praise was great, but in the back of my mind I was thinking about the second-round national tournament loss we were dealt at the end of that season. We had an excellent record of twenty-seven wins and just two losses, before that tournament loss. We were expected to go further into the tournament. But we lost early. That really bothered me.

In the national tournament loss, I only scored thirteen points. I was very disappointed in myself. I felt that if I was supposed to be such a good player, I should've been able to take my team further into the national tournament. After that loss I played the game in my mind, over and over again. I regretted not taking more shots. I felt like I should've had a bigger impact on the game.

I knew that the great players were supposed to lead their team to the promised land. I knew I had to do more the following season. I had to redeem myself for letting my team down. I began to think about the stories the seniors had told me about going to Salem, (destination of the final four) and how nice it was. I wanted to be the player to take my team to the final four.

As soon as the season was over I got back in the gym. Coach gave us a couple weeks off to recover after a long season, but I didn't want a break. I was already thinking about the upcoming season, and what I needed to improve on. I created my own workout routine, I gathered tapes from the previous season, and I started working out. I spent hours in the gym every day. I envisioned my team going deep into the tournament. I envisioned the fans being ecstatic about the success of the team. And I was going to find a way to do just that. I wanted to bring energy, and excitement back to the College of Wooster.

Setting a New Standard

My junior season of college basketball turned out to be one of the most stressful seasons of my career. The expectations were extremely high after having a strong sophomore season. And even though the expectations from fans were high, I had my own goals was determined to reach. That successful season made me hungrier for much more. My focus was primarily on team success that year.

My mind was set on improving my game even more. I wanted to really completely dominate every game that season. I started my off-season strong, by staying in Wooster instead of going back to Springfield for the summer. I talked to Coach Moore, and I explained to him how bad it was when I had gone home the previous year. He agreed that it would be better for me to stay in Wooster over the summer.

So he helped me get into the summer housing program on campus. I had to pay a small amount of rent, but it was well worth it. I was able to work all the summer camps, and events my coach hosted. And I was able to workout at our school gym. But even more importantly I was able to relax. No drama, no violence, no stress. Just me, the basketball, and the gym. I couldn't have been happier.

Coming into the season I had gotten even stronger than the year before. I continued my weight room routine. I continued to work on my game, and it continued to show on the court. I refused to allow the success from the previous year to go to my head. Instead of becoming big headed, I became hungrier. My success in the previous year made me want more. It made me thrive to be an even better player. I increased my bench press from 185 to 230, and I repped seven plates on each leg over thirty times on the leg press!

I watched game film from the previous season over the summer. I also stayed in shape by playing in local summer leagues. The leagues helped because I was able to get reps against other college players in the area. It was much more beneficial than working out alone.

Watching film, getting reps against other college players was vital to the upcoming season. I knew I would have a target on my back coming into the season. I knew that opposing teams, coaches, and fans would be coming for me every night. I knew I would face my opponent's best defender every game. So, I worked hard to make sure that I would be prepared for whatever came my way. There was no time for excuses.

All the articles in the paper, seeing my face all over campus, and the television commercial brought positive attention from the fans. But it made me a target for my opponents. They were determined to stop me from scoring. People were tired of hearing my name. I remember warming up for games and hearing people asking "which one is Cooper." Once they figured out who I was, they would rally the others to cheer against me.

I thought being in the spotlight was tough in high school, but it was nothing compared to college. My opponents knew a lot about me, and they would be anxious to use it against me. The opposing crowd would chant personal things about me before the game had even started. Then, during the game I faced my opponent's toughest defender. The loud chants and aggressive play from my opponent, made it tough to deal with. Those factors began to take a toll on me mentally.

To bring even more pressure, I was named first team Pre-Season All-America. The poll only selected five players in all of division three basketball in the United States! I was one of them. I was more than honored to make the pre-season team, but I also knew that it was going to draw even more attention to me. It gave my opponents another reason to come after me.

Still, I was determined to fight off whatever came my way. I knew it would be very challenging. And with the expectations from fans, and scheming by my opponents, it made things even tougher. My junior season would be the first time in my college career that I faced double teams on a consistent basis. The opposing coach would send an extra defender to guard me to make it tougher to score. As soon as I started to make a move, a help side defender would sprint toward me forcing me to get rid of the ball.

But I had already prepared myself for it over the summer. I knew they would come after me. Instead of shying away I accepted the challenge. I would walk onto my opponents' court, hours before the game and visualize the rowdy crowd yelling at me. I knew I had to mentally prepare myself for the chaos. From there I turned into an angry competitor. It was the only way I could combat their antics. If I allowed the crowd to get to me I would not be able to help my team.

It became a routine to arrive at the gym, hours before the game was set to start, and see my opponent's fans lined up ready to taunt me. And each time I would take it all in. I would remember their harsh words during the game and take it out on their players. I made it a point to come out and ferociously attack the defense. After a couple of big buckets, I would go on a rampage. But even during the midst of all the chaos, I made sure to stay composed. I couldn't allow the crowd to make me play out of control. Even though I played with integrity, I would never let up.

Having that mentality helped me persevere through most of the challenges. I was mentally prepared because I was so hard on myself. I refused to let up. I refused to fail. That mindset would pay off for both me and my teammates, as we went on to have one of the best seasons in school history.

Redemption!

We finished the season, as the conference champions for the third year in a row. We then, went on to win the conference tournament championship. Winning the conference tournament was even bigger than winning the season championship. We had lost the championship game, on our home floor by just two points two years in a row! Imagine watching your opponent cut down the nets on your own home floor, two years in a row. Imagine being that close and coming up short by two points, in a such a big game. That was more than enough motivation to want win.

I was more motivated than ever to help my team win that game after being so close. I remember sitting in the locker room before the game. It was one of the most intense moments of my career. I sat quietly and thought about us losing by two points to Wittenberg in that same game two years straight. I thought about the way I felt after we lost those games.

I blamed myself for not doing enough to lead my team to victory. I had even asked myself if I am supposed to be such a great player, how am I allowing my team to lose two years in a row? To the same team? I was angrily frustrated before the game had even started. Just the thought of losing again frustrated me. There was no way I could allow my team to lose that game again.

I had my mind made up that I would come out swinging. I had to help my team win this game. I had to set the tone. I was determined to take this game over. Psychologically, I was preparing myself for the fight of my life. At the jump ball my adrenaline was so high that I felt like my heart was about to come out of my chest. It was difficult to stand still while we waited for the game to start.

We were matched up against Ohio Wesleyan, after they had beaten Wittenberg in the semi-finals. And we were playing them in front of a sellout crowd on our home court. I remember our school spirit team creating a white t-shirt theme for the game. I remember looking into the crowd and seeing nothing, but white Wooster t-shirts all throughout the gym. Parents, kids, fans, and alumni had all bought into the theme.

We had just beaten Ohio Wesleyan in a close game a week before, so we knew it was going to be an intense battle. Just knowing the game was expected to be close motivated me even more. I didn't care what the crowd expected though. It was time to put up or shut up at that point. Talking meant nothing.

The start of the game was just as I anticipated. Both teams standing at center court, the crowd already in a frenzy. Fans on both sides were jumping up and down, yelling as loud as possible. Both teams, coaches, and fans anxious to see the outcome. It came down to whoever wanted it more. Grit and mental toughness would decide who the conference tournament champion would be. The winner would also claim the automatic bid into the national tournament.

As soon as the ball was tossed in the air I went into my zone. I scored our first two points of the game, on our first possession. I then, went on to score twenty-two points in the first half! I scored from the three, off the dribble, in the paint, and off of mid-range jumpers. I only missed one shot the entire first half! We had such a large lead that I barely played the second half.

We ended up winning the championship game by thirty-five points. And after scoring a game high twenty-six points, I was named MVP of the conference tournament! That was an excellent feeling to finally win that game. Especially after losing two years in a row. We were finally holding the conference championship trophy on our way to the national tournament.

That game was only the beginning of what was to come that season. Now it was time to prepare for the national tournament. The tournament we had worked so hard for. The tournament that gave us the opportunity to become national champions. I was more ready than I had ever been in my life. I had practiced my entire life for opportunities like this. I was prepared both mentally and physically to compete for a national championship.

We won our first three games of the national tournament, in blowouts not being tested at all. In the opening game, we got revenge on Transylvania. They beat us on their home court the year before to put us out of the national tournament. We were anxious to get revenge from last season's loss. We jumped out on them early and ended up beating them by twenty-six points. It was a great way to start the tournament.

We then beat Centre, another team from Kentucky, by seventeen points, then John Carroll by twelve.

Our first real test came against Brockport State, a team from New York. To make the game tougher, we had to play them in a gym that was thirty minutes from their hometown, which gave them home court advantage. The winner would go on to play in the final four in Salem. A place me and my teammates had dreamed about for two years.

Brockport State was loaded with talent. They were athletic, they had shooters, and they had size to go with it. Plus, they played very aggressively. Me and Rashad Harris were the featured headliners for the game. Everyone in the gym knew the game would be determined by which one of us had a better performance.

Brockport State had put together a game plan to stop me and we were focused on stopping Rashad. Rashad had just scored twenty-five points in the second half of their game the night before! He looked unstoppable. After getting in foul trouble he was forced to sit the first half, after scoring only four points. But he came back fiercely and scored half of his team's points in the second half to help them win.

Not only was this the game to lead either team to the final four, but it was the same game I had lost in high school. The regional final. We lost to Hamilton in the regional final game, during my senior season at South. That game was by far the worst loss I had ever taken on the basketball court.

I had never felt pain like that before the regional final loss in high school. Me and my teammates cried right there on the court, in front of thousands of people. The pain was too much to hide once reality hit and we knew our dreams of winning a state title were over.

As soon as the final buzzer went off and we had realized we lost, reality set in. That loss hurt me so much that I had contemplated quitting basketball. I never wanted to feel that pain again. We lost that game in high school because we let the pressure get to us. Instead of playing how we normally do, we came out stiff because we were overthinking the game.

At South we averaged over seventy-eight points per game throughout the year, but we only scored forty-five points in the loss. We played horribly. We had the worst shooting performance of the year, and we couldn't recover. I remember seeing my best friend, Isaiah Carson lay lifelessly on the floor following that loss. No one talked the entire ride home. We were all stunned about the turnout of that game. The team who had beaten us was going to the state tournament, we were going home. That was a triple dose of reality.

That game in high school was all I thought about while sitting in the locker room waiting to play Brockport State. I could not allow my team to lose in the regional final again. The loss in high school was more than enough incentive. This was a chance to redeem myself. I was going to do whatever I could to lead my team to victory.

I was normally mild mannered on the court. I rarely ever showed any emotion, but this game was different. It was personal. This was more than just another game. It was the biggest game of my career at that point.

You could tell it was a special game because of the energy and emotions we were playing with. As soon as I scored my first bucket, I exploded with excitement. And the fact that the crowd was really into the game brought more intensity from both teams. Fans, parents, and family members packed the small gym in Rochester, New York to watch us battle it out. The sold-out gym was so loud that we couldn't hear coach during the game. We had to create signals for plays to communicate our game plan.

Brockport State was a very good team. Plus, Rashad Harris was even better then what we had anticipated. He was extremely fast and he could shoot, which made it nearly impossible to stop him. We were behind most of the game. Even falling behind by more than ten points a few times. But we kept our composure.

Still, I refused to panic. I paced myself until the last five minutes of the game. That was when I gave it all I had, and brought my team back. I told myself that I would capitalize on every mistake they made and find a way to lead us to victory. We battled it out the first forty minutes, but the game was still tied after Brockport State missed a shot at the buzzer.

Now we are in overtime. Both teams are standing at center court waiting to start the overtime period. I walk over to my teammate Tom Port and told him we were winning that game. Brockport State had given us a second chance, and I was determined to take the game over. There was no way we were going to let them win after they missed that shot in regulation.

As soon as the ball went into the air I went into killer mode. The ball somehow landed in my hands after the tip, and I scored within a matter of seconds. They scored on the other end, then I scored again. I kept my determination and held onto the momentum. I ended up scoring nine of my teams thirteen points in overtime to lead us to the win and into the Final Four!

That was the best moment of my basketball career at that point. We did it! We had gotten past the regional final! We were finally going to the final four! I was so happy that I nearly cried tears of joy. It took me hours to settle down once the game was over. My emotions running extremely high during the game made it difficult to settle down. I couldn't believe we had actually made it to the final four! Winning that game was another one of my childhood dreams! I remember visualizing playing in games like that in elementary school.

We all ran around the gym celebrating, screaming, and yelling after the big victory. After finishing the game with a season high thirty-four points, the media announced on the loud speaker that I was named MVP of the Great Lakes Section! I had just been named the most valuable player in Ohio, Michigan, Kentucky, Indiana, and New York! It was unexpected, yet a great surprise. Our crowd roared even louder, after hearing the announcement on the loud speaker. I couldn't have been more excited after that win.

That was the moment I had worked so hard for. The moment I had dreamed about as a small child. I don't think I ever smiled that hard in my life! Unfortunately, my flash of glory was short lived. Initially I was caught up in the moment. I was running around the gym celebrating until I realized that I didn't have any family to celebrate with. I was the only player on the team who did not have any family in New York for the tournament.

Standing at the half court line I looked around and noticed every one of my teammates had family there to celebrate with. Everyone except me. For a second I started feeling terrible. I started to slip into that depressed mode, but I snapped out of it. It hurt but I couldn't allow myself to be unhappy. I forced myself to hide the pain and the embarrassment. Especially in front of all those people. I focused on the fact that we had just won a very important game. The biggest game of my career. That was all I allowed myself to think about.

I then left the court to answer questions during the press conference as if nothing was bothering me. I refused to allow anyone to see my true feelings. Plus, we had to play in the final four in a couple days. There was no time for self-pity. And even though it hurt I knew there was nothing I could do to change it. So I kept pushing forward. I forced myself to think about other things. Anything that would occupy my mind from dealing with the pain. And it worked. For the time being.

Once we arrived in Wooster from New York, we had one day to pack and get back on the road to Salem. We went through a brief practice, showered up, and got on the bus to get back on the road. As we were heading to the bus to leave for Salem we were greeted by approximately a hundred of our fans. The fans were standing outside of the team bus with signs cheering us on the way to Salem. That was a very special moment. To see people so enthusiastic about the teams' success, made me feel good to be a part of something so positive.

Growing up in Springfield, I was used to people finding something negative to say whenever I had experienced success. It was never good enough. Majority of the people in my hometown were very negative. After experiencing it so much I had become accustomed to it. But when I played for Wooster everything was different. The fans showed support that I had never experienced before. I loved that feeling of being surrounded by positive people. People who wanted to see you win.

The whole trip to Salem felt like a dream. The road trip, the media, everything was more intense. I even completed my first interview on live television, before our first game. I also participated in my first press conference in front of a group of reporters. I remember five reporters asking me questions at once and not knowing which one to answer first. I had seen NBA players complete those types of interviews on television, but I had never experienced it myself.

The interviews and the media were great, but my favorite part of the trip was going to the schools in Salem interacting with the children. In their eyes, me and my teammates were celebrities. As soon as we walked through the elementary school doors the kids jumped up and down with excitement. Seeing the kids' faces light up was a special feeling.

We each took a group of kids and read a book to them. Even though none of the kids paid any attention, it was still fun to interact with them. Hearing the kids blurt out questions about basketball made the situation light. Once we were finished reading, the kids were allowed to ask us questions about our team. Coincidentally, all the kids asked the same questions. Each group asked who could dunk, and who the leading scorer was. We had a great time talking with them.

After visiting the schools, it was time to get some rest for the game the following day. As soon as I had entered the arena on game day I felt the rush. It was the biggest arena I had ever played in. It seated more than ten thousand spectators. Everything looked brand new. Brand new rims. Brand new seats in the arena. It even looked like there was fresh paint on the floor. Plus, the bleachers were custom built. I couldn't wait to get on the court and lead my team to the title.

This time I had extra motivation. Unlike New York, (where I didn't have any family there), I had a small cheering section supporting me for the game. My girlfriend, her mother, and my little brother, George all came to support me and my teammates. It was a great feeling to have support after feeling alone in New York.

It was great to have my girlfriend and her mom come, but it was even more special to have my little brother there. I was excited to play in such a big game with my thirteen-year-old brother in the stands watching. It felt good to have an opportunity to show my brother something positive.

It was great to see the smile on his face as he looked around the large arena. I could tell my brother was excited to be there. The only things we had ever seen growing up were negative. We didn't have any role models to show us anything positive. It was great to experience such a big moment with my little brother. I felt like it would motivate him to want to do better. To strive for more.

The atmosphere was even better than it was in New York. The only difference was we were playing for something bigger, in a much larger gym. Me, and my teammates could not have asked for more support. We had the largest crowd out of the four teams that made it to the final four that year.

However, we fell behind early and ended up losing the game. I was battling two extreme forms of emotion after the loss. The competitor in me was devastated. It hurt to walk through confetti, as the opposing team celebrated their victory. Then to make things worse, I had to participate in a press conference right after the game. I remember going to the press conference and not answering a single question. I was sick about the loss. I didn't feel like talking.

But at the same time, that experience is something I will never forget. Coming from little Springfield, there weren't many positive things to look forward to. There wasn't much hope for me growing up. And to be able to play in a game like that, really made me feel special. Playing in the Final Four, in that arena in front of thousands of people was unbelievable. Then to have my little brother watching was more than I could ever ask for.

More Tragic News Back at Home

My junior season turned out to be the most successful season, of my college career. I had never been to a final four before that season, and I had never played on a team who won twenty-nine games in a season. To make things better, I was finally apart of a team that had sincere support from local fans. Seeing the fans come out and send us off to Salem is something I will never forget. It felt like a dream seeing people cheering for us, standing outside, holding signs with our names on them, people smiling, and ecstatic about the success of the team. I couldn't have felt better. But that didn't stop the bad news from coming from Springfield.

It was around December of 2007, we were set to fly out to California to play in a tournament. I was very excited about the entire trip. I had never been to California before. Coach told us we would be playing in Pomona and Riverside, California. And once we were finished with the tournament we would visit Los Angeles, then head to Las Vegas. I had seen those cities on television, but never had the chance to visit. Just the thought of going gave me butterflies.

I remember sitting in my dorm room after practice, two days before we were set to leave for the trip. My phone rang, it was my mom calling me. When I answered the phone she didn't say anything. The silence on the phone told me something was wrong.

So I nervously waited for her to tell me the bad news. I already knew it was something bad by the way my mom was acting. She started talking and I could tell by the shaking in her voice that she had been crying. By this time, I'm starting to feel worse. Not only do I realize that its bad news, but now I'm actually afraid to hear what she is about to say.

She finally speaks and she tells me that my best friend, Isaiah Carson's brother, John Carson had been shot and killed. As soon as she finished the sentence my heart dropped! I didn't know what to say. I just sat there with tears in my eyes. I immediately started thinking about our childhood and when I first met John.

I was with my step-father playing basketball at the Rec. Back then, the Rec was one of the most popular spots to play basketball in Springfield. The first thing I noticed about John was his shoes. He was wearing the signature shoes of *Sam Cassell,* a pair of shoes I had really wanted. At that point I had no idea of who he was or how good of a basketball player he was. I was more focused on the shoes he was wearing. However, I would soon find out who John Carson was.

I remember my step-father telling me, "that's John Carson the best player in the city." Then he pointed to the boy who was close to my age and told me, "that's his brother Isaiah." That was the first time I had met Isaiah and John Carson. It definitely would not be the last time though.

The grown men were playing on the close end so me and Isaiah went to the other end to play. That was the first time me and Isaiah ever played one on one. I remember going up by eight points, but him coming back and beating me in a game to twelve. I couldn't believe he had beaten me! I was shocked because no other kid my age could play with me. I was used to beating kids my age easily. That loss was really bothered me! He was a little bit bigger, and he was relentless going to the rim.

After the game I noticed we also had the same taste in shoes. We both had on the black and white, *Shawn Kemps*. From that point on we became inseparable. We played basketball together just about every day. And we would stay over each other's house's on the weekends.

At Isaiah's mom's house is where I met John on a personal level. I quickly learned that you had to have thick skin if you planned on going over there. You would get ambushed with jokes as soon as you walked through the door. Nobody was safe. John would crack on anybody. And he would have everyone on the porch laughing at you. It was even funnier when people didn't know him that well. They would be confused to how a person could meet them for the first time and just start cracking jokes on them. It was all in fun though.

Once I figured out that, that's just how he was, I became more comfortable. I then began to join in on the cracking matches. We used to crack jokes for hours. To everyone else John Carson was a legend. He had the whole city coming to watch him play ball. To me he was like a big brother. A goofy older brother who made you tougher.

At that age I didn't fully understand how good he really was. As I had gotten older I started to realize what statistics were. I started to learn what scoring averages were and that opened my eyes to the legend that he really was.

I heard stories about John dunking in the seventh grade! I remember seeing him wow the crowd with his passes. He would shake defenders and finish them off with a flashy shot. Then he would throw a pass to himself and dunk the ball. After he did all of that he would dance down the court showboating. The game looked easy to John Carson. It looked like he was having fun.

I will never forget the story I heard about John during his freshman season at South. Apparently, Coach Ham was not sure if he should play John on varsity or junior varsity. So he had John dress on the junior varsity team, then play a few quarters of varsity ball. Well, after that one game on junior varsity John would showed Coach Ham and everyone else that he was more than ready for varsity ball.

During the first game of his high school career, John scored forty points in just three quarters of the junior varsity game! By Ohio high school rules, players are only allowed to play five quarters total each game night. So John was only allowed to play two quarters of varsity because he had already played three quarters during the reserve game. Well he must've still been hot from the junior varsity game. He went on to score twenty more points in the varsity game, in just two quarters of playing time!

From there John was the headliner on one of the best teams, in

Springfield South high history. He averaged more than twenty-five points per game, to go along with five to six assists per game. He proved himself to be one of the best players in the state of Ohio. As a result of his outstanding skills he was recruited by legendary coach, Bob Huggins to play basketball at the University of Cincinnati. He played alongside of future NBA players: Kenyon Martin, Ruben Patterson, Danny Fortson, and many other first round NBA draft picks. He even saw action as a freshman on a loaded Cincinnati team.

I had known John for most of my life. He was family to me. I was best friends with his little brother. So to hear news like that was devastating. I couldn't believe what I was hearing. After I hung the phone up I literally sat there for hours trying to figure out what I had just heard. I then texted my coach and told him I would not be at practice that day. There was just no way I could be around people after hearing about John.

After about two hours of trying to gather my thoughts I had to do something I never thought I would have to do. I had to put my feelings aside and find the strength to call Isaiah. I was literally sick to my stomach just thinking about it. I didn't want to hear him like that. I already knew he would be crushed. But I had to be there for my brother. I had to call. Isaiah had lost his younger brother, Bear in a fire and I missed the candlelight. So I had to come through for him this time.

Scared, I attempted to make the dreaded call. I remember my hands shaking as I picked the phone up to call. I was thinking of what I was going to say before he answered the phone. But after the phone started ringing I punked out and hung up. I remember arguing with myself in my mind "I can't do it. No you have to do it." So I tried again. And I punked out again. Now I'm making it worse. So the third time I forced myself to stay on the phone.

When Isaiah answered we both just sat on the phone. I told myself I would not bring up any details, so I kept it as simple as possible. I remember telling him "I heard what happened." It hurt to hear the pain in Isaiah's voice when he responded. He said five words that I will never forget. "They took both my brothers." Hearing him say those words sent pain through my body. It crushed me to hear him like that. I swear I felt the pain in my heart. The situation was so bad that I don't even remember hanging up. The trauma from the situation caused me to forget how we got off the phone.

It hurt. It hurt bad. That was definitely one of the worst phone calls I have ever had to make. At the same time, I was relieved that I made the call. I just wanted Isaiah to know that I really cared. Losing John affected me too. I never wanted to see my best friend or his family go through something like that. It's crazy that years later Isaiah would be coming to the hospital to return the favor when I lost my brother to gun violence. Those were dreadful moments. But that's what brothers do for each other.

CHAPTER **11**

Now or Never

AFTER ALL OF the events that had taken place during the first three years of my college career, I didn't think it was possible to be under more pressure. I didn't think I could be any more motivated. But I was wrong. The pressure before was nothing compared to what I was going to face during my last year of college ball.

Coming into my senior season my girlfriend of four years was pregnant. That added extra pressure. I felt like I really needed to have an excellent senior season in order to earn a professional contract overseas. At that point, that was my only means of providing for my family.

Before the season had started I was named first team Pre-Season All-America for the second year in a row. Plus, me and my teammates had a chance to win a school record of four consecutive conference championships. We also had a chance to become the first class to make four consecutive appearances in the national tournament. If we accomplished those things we would be the first team in school or conference history to do so.

Coming into my senior season, I heard it from fans of how I had a chance to break multiple records in both school and conference history. I read about it in newspapers. I read about it on the school website. I also had a chance to become the second player in school history to score over two thousand points. With all of that hanging over my head I knew I had to perform well. Being under intense pressure was an understatement for the way I was feeling. And this all came before the season had even started. I was stressed out of my mind!

To make it worse, the season started out rough. The expectations I put on myself were getting out of hand. I didn't realize that I was being too hard on myself until after the season. The pressure from fans didn't help. It had gotten to the point where scoring twenty points in a game was not enough. Everyone expected more. Plus, I was driving myself crazy trying to play on a level, I thought professional scouts were looking for.

Seeing my girlfriend's stomach grow only added more stress to the situation. I knew I had to provide for my daughter. My plan was to earn a professional contract in order to do so. It was the only thing I identified with. The only job I knew I was good at. So I pushed myself past extremes to get better. There was no way I was going to let my daughter down.

But the pressure I was putting on myself was becoming unbearable. It also started to affect how I performed on the court. Instead of being myself and playing aggressively, I started overthinking everything. I was afraid to make a mistake. I kept telling myself that if I did not play on a certain level I wouldn't make it overseas. No team would want me if I did not have a dominant senior season. I was way too critical of myself.

As a result of my own self-criticism I had two horrible games in a row. I scored eight points against Lake Erie, and nine points against Cedarville. To make it worse, we lost both of those games! That was the first time that we had ever lost two games in a row during my college career. It was also the first time I had not scored in single digits since my freshman season. To add to it we fell out of the top twenty-five in the national rankings for the first time in my college career. Everything seemed to be coming down on me at once. I felt like I had the weight of the world on my shoulders.

After those two horrible games I was averaging a pathetic, fourteen points per game (my lowest scoring average since my freshman season)! That was by far the lowest point of my college career. I was so weak mentally that I couldn't stand to look at myself in the mirror. I remember being ashamed. Being angry with myself for playing like a chump. I felt like I didn't recognize myself. I couldn't believe how bad I was playing.

It only made it worse that I wasn't the only person who noticed it. I had to hear it from my coach, I read about it on campus, and I had to see it in the newspaper.

After two long weeks of self-doubt, I found a way to bounce back. I refused to allow myself to continue to play on that level. It was embarrassing. I had to find a way to get back to my old ways. I became angry and came out with a vengeance. And once I had returned to myself I went on a rampage. I knew that I had a lot of catching up to do. I started by scoring thirty-two points against Ohio Wesleyan, I then scored thirty-two points the following game against Walsh. After that I scored twenty-four, and twenty-nine points in a tournament in the Bahamas. My scoring average was back to around twenty points per game and my confidence was lifted back up.

From there I would go on to have my most successful season of my college career. I averaged career highs in points per game, assists, and steals. I also scored my two thousandth point, and I was named an All-American for the third year in a row. I became the first player in school history to make the All-American team three times. And after all that stressing I played well enough to earn a professional contract to play in Dortmund, Germany.

CHAPTER 12

Jayda Nicole Cooper

WE WERE GETTING closer to the due date of my first-born daughter. The feelings I was experiencing were different than anything I had ever felt before. It was a love I had never felt for anyone else. It was strange that my feelings were so strong considering I had not even met my daughter yet. I would get butterflies just thinking about her arrival. I was extremely anxious to meet her.

All I could think about was being a better parent then what my parents were to me. I wanted to be the best father a little girl could ever ask for. Just the thought of my daughter being around made everything else irrelevant. Even basketball. My whole life I had depended on basketball to help me cope with life. But now that my daughter was coming she was all I cared about. All I could think about was spending time with her.

Jayda Nicole Cooper was due on March 6, 2008. Coincidentally I was scheduled to play in the national tournament game in Chicago on March 7, 2008. In my mind there was no question of where I was going to be. If the game schedule conflicted with the birth of my daughter, then I was going to miss the game. There was no way I would even consider missing the birth of my own daughter for anything. Especially not for a basketball game.

Coach Moore already knew where I stood on the situation. So he called me into his office a week before we were supposed to leave. When we met I reiterated that if my daughter was coming around the time of our trip, then I would not be attending. The news frustrated Coach Moore, but it also frustrated me. I felt like he wasn't being considerate of my situation. But to be fair it was a difficult situation for both sides.

I played a big part in helping our team win games. Plus, it was my senior season. So I understood where he was coming from. At the same time Coach Moore knew that I grew up without a father. I felt like he should've understood why I was so adamant about being there for the birth of my daughter.

Still, coach tried to persuade me to go with the team. Us disagreeing led to an argument. And after going back, and forth for a while Coach Moore suggested that I speak with the doctor to see if Jayda was breached yet (getting ready to come out). So we went and got the opinion of the doctor. I told them about my situation with the basketball trip and the doctor ensured us that Jayda most likely wouldn't be born before I came back. The trip would only last five days even if we won both games. That gave me plenty of time to get back. So I went with my team to Chicago.

Conflict on Game Day!

It was March 7, 2008, I was sitting in my hotel room in Chicago watching television. Coach called our room and told us it was time to load the bus for the game. As soon as I got up to grab my bag, my cell phone rang. I look at my phone and see the call is from Jayda's mom. I anxiously pick the phone up and to my surprise, Jayda's step grandmother is on the phone.

As we were talking I could hear Jayda's mom in the background screaming. As soon as I realized I was going to miss the birth of my daughter I lost it. My nerves were so bad that I could not hold onto the phone. My heart was pounding uncontrollably and my hands were shaking badly. I felt a rush of guilt, I felt sad, I felt like my heart was about to explode from all the stress and emotions I was feeling. I thought to myself, "how could I miss my own daughters' birth?" I started to panic. I couldn't sit still. My thoughts began to wonder all over the place. I had spent my whole life telling myself I would be nothing like my father. Then I turn around and miss the birth of my own daughter. I was so ashamed.

However, I had to force myself to snap out of that mindset. I had to man up and call back to see what was going on. So I walked into the stairway of the hotel to be alone. I called back and Jayda's step grandmother answered again, so I hung the phone up. I was angry with her because of lack of support. Jayda's step grandmother didn't call to check on her or offer any advice with the pregnancy, so we weren't on talking terms. And it made me even more angry that she was there and I wasn't.

I was extremely angry and hurt about the whole situation. It was tough to hold my emotions back as I had done before. I was so distraught that I started yelling in the stairway. So loudly that my teammates could hear me through the hallway. Once I walked back into the hallway they started asking questions about what was going on.

My teammates' parents' then started asking about the baby once I entered the elevator to load the bus. One of the moms asked me if Jayda had arrived yet. I reluctantly told them her mom was in labor. My teammates' parents' started cheering loudly as if it was a good thing. Not realizing that I was angry that I missed the birth of my own daughter. That frustrated me even more.

As I'm walking onto the bus on the way to the game; I am receiving pictures of my daughter through a cell phone! That made me very angry! I was supposed to be there with them! Instead I was five hours away getting ready for a basketball game!

I still couldn't believe I missed the birth of my daughter. I was having a really hard time suppressing the negative thoughts. My mind was all over the place. And no matter how hard I tried, I could not settle down. All I can think of, was the fact that I missed the birth of my daughter, after I had been waiting so long to meet her. I was so angry with myself that I was nearly in tears.

But just like old times I had planned to hide my emotions. I had to act like everything was okay even though I felt terrible. This time would be different though. Normally I would be able to put my feelings aside and perform well under the pressure. But missing the birth of my daughter brought a whole new level of pain and frustration. I couldn't shake the feeling of guilt. It was too much to deal with.

I remember being in the locker room while coach was going over the game plan, and not hearing a word he said. I was completely zoned out. He had told me my assignment for the night and I nodded as if I was ready, but I wasn't even thinking about the game. I had forgotten what coach had told me before we had even left the locker room. I was thinking about my daughter so much that I could not focus on the game.

We are at center court and the game is about to start. Any other time I would be anxious to start the game. I would be in a different mode, ready to compete. But I didn't have that fire this time. I didn't care as much. And it showed in my performance. I finished the first half with zero points, and even shot two air balls!

I was desperately trying to snap out of it, but I just could not focus on the game. At one-point, coach pulled me out of the game because of my performance. He was frustrated, yelling right in my face, but I did not hear a word he said. I was literally looking right through him thinking about my daughter. I just couldn't focus.

Once the first half was over and we were down by fifteen points I became fed up with the whole situation. I decided it was time to play. I had already missed the birth of my daughter, and if I didn't snap out of it, that was going to be my last game as a collegiate basketball player. So I came out of the locker room with the fire I normally had. I somehow mustered enough energy to have an impact on the game. I ended up scoring twenty-four points in the second half to bring us back, but it still wasn't enough.

We ended up losing the game, on top of me missing the birth of my daughter. After all of this going through my head, I had to face the reporters again. They asked me questions about the game and why I played so badly in the first half. Me not scoring in an entire half was unheard of. But I avoided all of the questions about my performance. I spoke on other parts of the game instead. I refused to give an excuse for why I played bad. I also did not want the reporters to know my personal business. So I answered as quickly as I could so I could get out of there.

Now it was finally time to head back to Ohio. I was finally on my way to see my daughter. I couldn't wait to get on the bus so that I could head home. But unfortunately I ran into a problem that would delay me getting back to her.

There was a really bad snow storm that came through Ohio and Illinois over the weekend. It caused closures on the highways in certain parts of Ohio. Because of the storm we were only allowed to travel to Toledo. From there everything was shut down. We ended up being stuck in Toledo for two days. I sat in the hotel room bored, anxiously waiting to get back to hold my daughter.

When I finally made it back to Wooster, I didn't wait in the locker room. I didn't even go home to change clothes. I went straight to the hospital to meet my daughter. I ran in the room, dropped my bags on the floor, and picked my daughter up. The feelings I was experiencing were indescribable.

I felt adrenaline, excitement, fear, but most of all love. I couldn't believe I played a part in making such a beautiful baby. When I finally got the chance to hold her I just sat there, and stared at her beautiful little face. I couldn't believe that beautiful baby girl was mine. I instantly fell in love with her.

As I held her I began to think about my childhood. I wondered how any parent could leave their child? How could my dad leave me and not care? How can you not fall in love with your own child? That first moment of holding my daughters hand was very special to me. Feeling her tiny, little hand grip my finger is something I will never forget. It was a feeling I had never felt before. I told myself that I would always be there for her.

The next couple of months seemed to fly by quickly. My whole world was revolved around raising my daughter and finishing school. Basketball had really become a third priority, especially considering my college career was over. If I wasn't in class I was spending time with my daughter. Her mother was working as a student teacher while I was still school. So it was just me and Jayda during the day.

I was on daddy duty full time and I loved it. It didn't bother me one bit. I loved being a father. In my mind I was doing what any responsible father would do. Playing with her, feeding her, changing diapers, burping her, and rocking her to sleep. It was all part of my daily routine.

I loved every minute of it. Taking care of my daughter made me feel like I had a bigger purpose in life. I brought her with me everywhere I went. I even took her to the cafeteria with me sometimes. And when I had to drop her off to go to class I missed her like crazy.

CHAPTER 13

Living a Dream

AFTER SPENDING A couple months taking care of my daughter, I had to get back to business. For the time being, my only priorities were going to class and looking after Jayda. I had not touched a basketball or been in the weight room in over two months! I remember going to the gym and feeling fatigued from just shooting around. I was in really bad shape. Plus, I had gained more than twenty pounds from just sitting around. But I knew I would get back into my groove in no time. Looking at my daughter every day was all the motivation I needed.

I had dreamed of being a professional basketball player ever since I was in the first grade. Now it was finally time to pursue it. I had shopped around for weeks trying to find the best agent. And after choosing an agent I began negotiating with professional teams in Iceland, Germany, and Japan. I was working to find the best contract for me and my family. During that time, I had also sent my information to a couple of NBA teams to see if I could get a response. I knew it was a long shot, but I figured it wouldn't hurt to try.

I sent tapes, and my statistics to team scouts all over the NBA. And to my surprise the Orlando Magic replied. They spoke of me possibly playing for their summer league team. I had also received responses from the Cleveland Cavaliers, and the Memphis Grizzlies. But they were not willing to give me a shot.

Still, just seeing the NBA logo on the emails was enough to get me worked up. I was so excited that I couldn't sleep at night. Nothing came out of it though. The Magic chose a taller guard for their summer league team. The Cavaliers, and Grizzlies acknowledged that my shooting percentages were exceptional, but didn't invite me in for a workout.

From there my next best option was Japan. When my agent had first sent the contract I immediately sent it back and asked if there was a misprint. I was certain that she had sent the wrong information, but she assured me it was accurate. Believe it or not we were negotiating for a contract worth $30,000/month to play basketball in Japan, in their top league. I never had that much money in my life! I couldn't believe what I was reading.

Seeing the contract motivated me to work even harder. I was determined to give myself a better chance of being picked up by one of the teams in Japan. But after a month of negotiating the league president advised me to play in a lower level league to prove myself first. I was naive at that time, but I later learned that the professional teams wanted big men first. As a guard, you had to prove you were good enough to play on a professional level before they would sign you to a large contract.

So I was forced to look at other options for my first year of professional basketball. Iceland was one of the first leagues to contact me, but it seemed like a weird place to live. I knew up front that I most likely would not end up playing there. Once they had told me about the time format, I had even more doubts.

Apparently, Iceland does not have the time format that we have in America. Their format consists of six months of darkness, and six months of light. So it would be dark outside for the entire day for six months straight. Then it would be light outside for six months straight. It didn't help that the league did not look as competitive as the other leagues overseas.

So I continued to negotiate with teams in Germany. Germany had a great basketball market with great benefits. After about a month of negotiating I decided to sign with Dortmund SVD 49ers, located in Dortmund, Germany. I immediately started doing research on the city to get familiar with my new home. I found out that the population in Dortmund, was 760,000! Dortmund was the fifth largest city in Germany at that time. That was a huge difference from the 55,000 population I was accustomed to. The city was more than ten times larger than Springfield and Wooster.

After signing the contract, I had a few months before I was scheduled to leave. So I decided to move back home to Springfield for those two months. But even though I was living back home I made sure to stay away from all of the drama and chaos. I was either in the house playing with my daughter, working out, or at my moms' house talking to my brother.

Me and my brother started working out together on a daily basis. My main focus wasn't working out though. It was more about us bonding as brothers. I knew I was going to be gone for a while, so I wanted to spend time with my brother before I left. Plus, it gave us time to talk about life.

I didn't want my brother to go through the things I had gone through. I talked to him about making better decisions than the ones I made. I also talked to him about getting out of Springfield. I'm sure he was tired of hearing me say it, but I didn't care. I knew there was nothing but trouble back home.

Having Second Thoughts

It came time for me to leave for Germany, but I had mixed feelings. It was strange because this was my dream. I had dreamed about playing professional basketball my entire life. But now that it was time to pursue it, I was hesitant. Playing basketball wasn't the problem though, it was leaving my daughter. I couldn't face the thought of leaving my her behind. That was the toughest part. Plus, I would have to miss my brother play football.

But it was time to leave, rather I was ready to go or not. I was making my rounds through the city saying my goodbyes to family and close friends. I decided to stop by my moms' house last before I headed to Cleveland to fly out. I had given my mom a hug first. I remember having to remind myself to be strong. I knew that if I had broken down they would too. That would only make the situation worse. Still it was very difficult to keep my composure. It was even tougher when I walked up to the house and noticed that my mom had tears in her eyes. That was enough to break me down right there.

I figured I would just say goodbye quickly and get in the car before anyone started crying. Already fighting tears, I walked over to give my brother a hug, but before I even had a chance to he burst out crying. He started crying uncontrollably. My brother was crying so hard that it made mom cry. That really made it difficult for me to leave. I had never seen my brother cry that hard before. It really bothered me seeing him like that.

I remember him yelling that he did not want me to leave. His face full of tears, sobbing as he tried to talk. That hurt. That hurt bad. I stood there fighting to hold back the tears. I couldn't get over how my brother had reacted. At that point I really thought about staying back. But then again how was I going to take care of my family, if I turned that money down? I honestly didn't want to leave, but I had to.

After reluctantly leaving my mom's house I had to drive to Cleveland, and get on the plane. The whole three-hour drive I dreaded having to face my daughter at the airport. The whole time we were driving I thought about how difficult it was going to be to leave Jayda behind. I knew saying goodbye was going to be scarier than the flight itself.

We arrived at the airport. They walked with me until I got to the gate. As we had gotten closer to the gate I started to walk slower. I figured I would slow the process as much as possible because I really didn't want to leave my daughter. I couldn't stand to look at her innocent little face and say goodbye.

We reached the gate, and before I can even say a word Jayda's mom starts crying. I tried to keep my composure, so I turned and looked at Jayda. She was just staring at me not aware of what was going on. I knew I could not hold my tears much longer. So I quickly hugged them and walked off before Jayda caught on to what was happening. I don't know how I did it, but I held my tears until I got away from them.

Seeing my brother react that way was bad enough. Then I had to look at my daughter and say goodbye. I started to wonder if playing basketball was really worth it. Seeing my family break down was a lot to deal with. It really broke me down for a minute. It was difficult, but I fought through it and refocused on doing what was best for my family.

After a long flight I finally arrived in Germany. It was time to get to work. I had no idea that living there would be so challenging though. The basketball part was fine. I had seen just about everything on the court, so there wasn't much that would surprise me.

However, living in a foreigner country was a different story. Everything was a challenge. Ordering food, finding the practice facility, getting home from practice, even going to the grocery store was difficult. And the task of trying to speak German was nearly impossible. Everything was difficult for me in Dortmund.

Once I arrived everything seemed to be happening so fast. I was taking in so much information that it was beginning to drive me crazy. There was so much to learn in such a small amount of time. I had to learn where I could get groceries, where I could shop for clothes, and even how to get home from practice.

It was even difficult trying to pronounce the German language. I had to speak in German to get anything accomplished because no one spoke English. It was very challenging because their words were very long and difficult to pronounce.

I also had trouble getting used to their food. It was disgusting. The language and the food were enough to deal with. But the biggest factor was that I was missing my daughter. I thought about her every day. Before leaving for Germany there wasn't a day that I did not spend with my daughter. I went from seeing her every day to being on different parts of the world not able to see her at all. I couldn't walk into the next room and pick her up anymore. That was really starting to get to me.

Jayda eventually ended up coming over to Germany, but basketball just wasn't the same for me. I couldn't get up for a game the way I used to after my daughter was born. Being a positive example for Jayda was all I cared about. That was my main focus. I was also worried about her safety while living in Germany. The closest hospital was about thirty minutes away. I was worried that if my daughter had gotten sick that it would take too long to get there.

It made it worse that our away games would take up the entire day. In my first away game I was gone for over nine hours! I instantly started contemplating if it was worth it or not. What if something happened to them while I was away at a game? How could I protect them being that far away? The stress of being in a foreign country with a baby, and the lack of love for the game was enough for me to give it up. I returned home to Springfield to start over.

CHAPTER 14

Back in Springfield

AFTER THINGS DIDN'T work out in Germany I figured I would come back home, and build a life in Springfield. That was a very bad decision. I knew how bad my experiences were before, but I had hoped it would be different this time. I couldn't have been more wrong. I quickly learned that I had made a huge mistake going back home.

When I had first come back home I decided I would help my mom and my siblings. Growing up my family had struggled with finances. Different utilities were cut off at different times, food was limited, we just never knew what was going to go wrong from day to day. It was a very challenging experience growing up that way.

But now that I was in a position to help my family, I jumped on the opportunity. I helped my mom pay bills, I gave my siblings money, gave rides, and did other things to help out. The problem was I spent more money than I had planned to. And I spent it quickly. I spent more than three thousand dollars in a month!

I had to cut back or else I would put my own family in a bad spot. But once I had stopped catering to my family, they expressed their true feelings about me. As soon as I told them no, we started having issues. My younger sisters were quick to tell me that we weren't real siblings and that they did not acknowledge me as their brother.

Even though our family was never close, it didn't feel good to hear that. It really bothered me at first, but in the long run it taught me a lesson. Why help someone who doesn't care about you? If they felt that way, then why bother being around them? Apparently I was only their brother when I doing something to benefit them.

So I stepped away for a little while. I quickly noticed that things had not changed within my family. Everyone was still selfish and focused on drama. There were problems every day within our family. Someone arguing, someone talking bad about their own sibling, even competing with each other. It was too much to deal with.

After struggling to find a job in Springfield, I decided I would go back and finish school. I figured it would increase my chances of getting a better paying job. I later found out that with a Bachelor's degree, I could work as a substitute teacher. I had completed all of the requirements for my Bachelor's degree except for a foreign language. Once I completed that I would have my degree and be able to teach.

In the meantime, life was getting worse. Me and my girlfriend had split up after our return to Springfield. She went to live with her mom in Northridge and I ended up staying with my biological father, of all people.

Fighting to Get Ahead

My father had gotten addicted to crack and was not doing well. I noticed it during my freshman year of college. I was home on break and I had seen him walking down an alley. His appearance had changed so dramatically I had to ask my mom if that was my dad or not. He had lost so much weight that his face had become very thin. I was used to seeing his heavy set frame of about two hundred pounds. My dad probably weighed a hundred and forty pounds when I had seen him. He was barely recognizable.

I was home during spring break the following year when I ran into one of my dad's friends. He had told me that my dad was fighting to get his life back in order. He also stated that he thought it would motivate my dad if I had gone to see him. To be honest, I was still frustrated with my father. I was angry that he was never there when I was a kid. I was also frustrated that he never explained why he left me. At the same time, I did not hate my father. And if me going to see him motivated him, I felt I should do what I could to help. So I agreed to go see him.

After going to see him, my dad and I agreed to try to mend our relationship. We ended up staying in contact periodically after I went to go see him. He even attended a few of my college games after we started talking again. And after I returned home from Germany our conversations continued. When I returned home, things got out of control and I ended up asking my dad if I could stay with him until I saved up enough money to move out.

I stayed with my father for about eight months. The living conditions were not the best, but I had nowhere else to go. To add to my frustration there was barely any food in the house. Plus, my dad and his girlfriend both smoked cigarettes. I hated cigarettes, but I was forced to deal with the smell since I was living in his house. Those living conditions added to my motivation to finish school and get out on my own.

The living conditions were bad, but there were other issues that bothered me more. I had always been curious to why my father was absent during my childhood. I just didn't know how to bring it up without it leading to confrontation. It was an awkward situation altogether. I figured he would get defensive and we would end up arguing, so I left it alone. But now that we were living in the same house I thought about it more. I wondered how he could leave me and just go on with his life.

That was until me and my father got into a heated argument. I had caught my father talking behind my back to his girlfriend. That situation went south quickly. The argument went from us arguing about him talking behind my back to my childhood. Which only made things worse.

My father insisted that he tried his best to be there for me. In his mind he had done enough because he paid child support. That really pissed me off hearing my father justify his reasons for not being there. I couldn't believe what I was hearing. I couldn't believe he had the nerve to sit there and justify why he left. As a kid I desperately needed a father in my life.

It made me angrier hearing him speak with confidence about why he left. He claimed he had to leave Springfield in order to live a decent life. He obviously didn't care about my well-being. I needed a father! Especially the way we were living with mom. Having a father who cared for me and loved me would have changed my whole perspective on life. It would've given me more confidence. It would've given me hope for a decent future. Guidance.

I grew up feeling like I wasn't good enough. I struggled with self-esteem issues throughout my entire childhood. I had no direction in my life besides basketball. I had no back-up plan for my life. No one to protect me. No one to lead me in the right direction.

Instead I was forced to take on responsibilities of a grown man at the age of nine! It really made me angry that my father did not understand my frustration. Having a father to teach me, and show me how to be a man would've changed everything!

As I expressed these things to my father I continued to get angrier. Just thinking about my horrible childhood and how he could've saved me from most of the suffering made me furious. The argument carried on and it got really heated. It had gotten to the point where I could see a fight coming between us. And if my father would've challenged me I was going to punch him out. I had reached my breaking point. I was tired of hearing all of his excuses. All I wanted was for him to be honest. I couldn't get those years back. The least he could've done was admit that he abandoned me.

But he didn't. Instead he kept talking about the child support he claimed he was paying. I told my father that even if he did pay child support he still wasn't there for me. Paying child support did not make him a father in my eyes. I really didn't believe he had ever paid child support anyway. My father insisted he did and it only made me angrier.

During the argument my father stormed off with tears in his eyes. He went upstairs and brought back a stack of papers. He then handed me the papers, tears still in his eyes. The papers were documents proving that he had been paying child support most of my life. As soon as I read the documents my heart dropped! I was still angry with my father for not being there, but my focus was now on my mom.

Seeing those papers changed the way I looked at my mom. I was disgusted with my mother. I felt anger, extreme pain and betrayal all at the same time. I could not believe she had been lying to me for twenty-four years about not receiving child support! I felt like I didn't know who she was. How could a person do that to their own child? How can a person keep a lie going for that long? I couldn't believe it! I just couldn't believe what I had just read! My feelings were crushed!

I started thinking about all the times we struggled as kids. I thought about the times my mom would ask me for money for bills when I was in college. I was giving her money that I didn't have because I didn't want my siblings to suffer. Meanwhile she was getting child support and lying about it the whole time!!! Keeping the money that was supposed to be coming to me! I thought about the time I bought my siblings Christmas one year after my mom claimed she didn't have the money. To find out it was all a lie made me feel a sense of anger I never felt before.

I sent my mom money for bills on numerous occasions when I was in college. I even paid my own tuition over the summer by working summer camps because she said she didn't have money to help. I couldn't believe my mom could be so selfish. I was so hurt that I couldn't think straight. I was hoping the papers were false. It was very difficult to take that in. I refused to believe it. So I called my sisters to see if it was true.

I called my sister Heather first. I asked her if mom was getting child support for me and she replied, "mom has been getting child support for you, you didn't know?" I couldn't believe what my sister had just told me. So I called my other sister Vashawna and she said the same thing. I couldn't believe what I was hearing! Everybody knew except me. My mom had been getting money for me every two weeks, but not giving me a penny of it. And then turning around asking me for money. I felt stupid for trusting my mom.

After waiting a couple of days I finally confronted my mom. And she did just what I expected her to do. Play the victim and turn it around on me. She acted as if she had no idea what I was talking about. So I got the papers from my father and showed them to her. I asked her how could she lie to me for all those years. But instead of answering she went around the question.

She started an argument saying I was disrespectful to her. So not only did she lie, but she refused to explain why she did it. Starting the argument was her way of dealing with the situation. She knew that if she had turned the focus to something else that she would not have to deal with what she had done. I was in disbelief of everything that had just taken place. I was so hurt that I didn't speak to my mom for about a month after that incident. I was crushed.

From that point on, my family had continued to be the main source of drama in my life. I was just too young and too dumb to separate myself from them. Whenever something happened my mom called me and I came running. Whenever my sisters called I came running. After having so many problems within our family I began to expect drama every time my phone rang. Nobody in my family ever called just to talk or to see if I was okay. They called to borrow something or to tell me who I needed to confront about a problem. A few incidents had really gotten out of hand.

Getting Out of Hand

I remember being at my friend's house watching television when my phone rang. My sister Kyera called me, but I did not answer. I figured she was calling to tell me about something negative so I ignored it. But after she called three times consecutively I knew something was wrong. The fourth time she called, I reluctantly answered the phone.

As soon as I picked up the phone I heard a bunch of screaming and yelling. So much that I couldn't understand what they were saying. I had to scream into the phone for them to talk one at a time, so I could understand them. Still, all I could understand was that my sister Darrien had gotten into a fight. And when she was fighting the stroller had gotten knocked over with Kyera's son in it.

I then rushed over to Keifer where the fight had taken place. When I pulled up to see what was going on there was a crowd of people standing in the street. But I didn't see anyone in my family. Then all of the sudden my brother comes storming out of the crowd covered in blood! He was bleeding all over, crying. I couldn't believe what I was seeing. Seeing all that blood scared me.

My first thought was he had gotten stabbed. So I yelled at my brother to get in the car. I then asked him what happened. He explained to me that he told Darrien not to fight the girl because she had Sincere (Kyera's son) with her. But Darrien started fighting the girl anyway.

The fight escalated quickly and he could not break them up. So he had gotten frustrated and punched out the window of the car. When he hit the window the glass cut him. I was still frustrated, but it was a relief to know that my brother had not been stabbed. He still lost a lot of blood though.

So now I'm driving my brother to the hospital and the phone rings (he had taken Darrien's phone during the fight). The caller was the girl who Darrien was fighting earlier. She was calling to keep the fight going. So, me thinking out of anger took the phone from my brother and asked where she was at. I then pulled up to her house and got out of the car. I made my brother stay in the car and called George-Ann (my sister) and told her to fight the girl who called the phone.

The fight erupted again. But after a while I pulled George-Ann off the girl. That's when I noticed Darrien was fighting again. So I went over to Darrien and made her go to the car too. As I was making Darrien leave, one of the girls ran up behind my mom as if she was going to hit her. I quickly tossed her out of the way. The girl then threatened to get her brother.

I'm still worked up so I walk across the street and wait for him to come expecting a fight. The girls brother goes into the house instead of confronting me and grabs a gun. Now he is coming to the car with the gun in his hand. I panic and speed off to get away. The whole time all of this is going on my brother is screaming, scared telling me how he doesn't want me to die. The whole situation had gotten completely out of hand.

After driving off I took my brother to the hospital. We ended up being at the hospital for more than five hours, while he got his hand stitched. As I sat in the hospital I thought about how everything had happened so fast. I thought about how dumb I was for getting involved in all of my family's issues. I thought about how I would've been the one who had gotten shot. How my daughter would be left without a father? It didn't make any sense and I knew it was time for a change. The drama was getting out of hand and it was only a matter of time before something serious happened.

Meanwhile I had not seen my daughter in months! It was driving me crazy. After me and Ashley split up she decided to try to keep Jayda away from me. She knew how important Jayda was to me, so she used my daughter as a way to get back at me. Her parents had coached her through the situation telling her she had majority of the rights to our daughter.

Their plan worked though. Not being able to see my daughter had nearly driven me crazy. I had begun to lose my mind. I no longer had an appetite. I had trouble sleeping and I started spending most of my time alone. I didn't want to be around anyone. I just wanted to deal with my problems alone.

I wouldn't go down without a fight though. I figured out how to file paperwork for rights to my daughter. It took longer than expected, but it paid off. I was eventually awarded partial visitation with Jayda. I was set to have time with my daughter every other weekend. I was very excited to be able to spend time with Jayda. She was very special to me. She motivated me to want to be a better person for her.

CHAPTER **15**

A Positive Reason to Come Back

MY PERSONAL LIFE in Springfield had always been rough. It was one of the reasons I wanted to get away so badly. Coming back to Springfield opened my eyes to why I was so determined to leave in the first place. There was a constant reminder of drama that seemed to occur every day. I had gotten tired of that lifestyle. However, there was one bright spot about coming back. That was watching my younger brother play football on Friday nights. It was a sight to see.

Growing up I knew my brother was going to be an exceptional athlete. I remember watching him do back-flips in the front yard at the age of seven. He was also very fast to be a chubby kid. My brother was the total opposite of me. I was unsure of myself, so I second guessed everything I was involved in. George, on the other hand was fearless. He would jump into things head first without thinking twice. Everything seemed to come to him naturally.

I can still remember my first season of playing organized basketball and how afraid I was. Everything about the game intimidated me. It took a disappointing season to get me going. In George's first season of organized football it looked like he was born to play the sport. The crowd, the chaos, and all the noise did not bother him. I remember being amazed at how he could run the football. He had speed to outrun opponents, he was thick enough to run them over, and he had moves that made it difficult to tackle him.

By the age of nine, my brother had already made a name for himself on the football field. George played running back and linebacker for the Springfield Broncos, pee wee football team. I remember our whole family traveling to watch him play. It was exciting to watch my little brother thrive on the football field. He put on a show every game.

The league my brother played in created a mercy rule for the weaker teams in the league. The president of the league did not want teams to lose too badly, and hurt the kid's confidence. So they put in a rule that if a team won by more than thirty-five points, the organization would be fined by the league. That way the coaches would be reluctant to run the score up. This affected my brother because they had to limit how many times he touched the ball. George was so good that he scored nearly every time he ran the ball.

So every game my brother received the first hand off of the game. And believe it or not, George scored on that first run ninety percent of the time. The coaches wanted to get him the ball early to make sure he would have a chance to run the ball. Otherwise it would be risky to let him run late in the game. Especially if they were already winning. Giving him the ball late in the game would most likely result in him scoring which would lead to the team getting fined. I remember one of the coaches telling my mom that my brother had scored forty-seven touchdowns, in just fifteen games!

George was an excellent pee wee football player. And even though he had started off strong, no one could have predicted what he was going to do in high school! George was naturally a running back, but his arm strength was incredible, so they made him play quarterback in middle school. He came into high school, and earned the job as the starting quarterback on the varsity team as a freshman. The sky was the limit.

This is where he really began to show how talented he was. In the first two years of varsity football he played quarterback, he returned kicks, and even played safety. But once they had put him back at his natural position at running back, he really began to flourish. I remember being amazed at what he could do with the ball in his hands. I was the older brother, but I was a fan of my little brother. He was twice the athlete I was. I couldn't do the things he was doing. I was just proud to be able to witness it.

I remember meeting up with my friends being anxious to watch my brother play on Friday nights. We would travel all over central and southwest Ohio to watch him play. And he put on a show every time he stepped on the field. After making spectacular plays every week my brother earned the nickname "wiggles" because of the way he moved with the ball in his hands. He would change directions quickly, reverse the field, spin, break free, and outrun everyone on the field for a touchdown. It was really special to watch my brother play the game.

You could tell by watching that it was more than just football for him. I knew from experience how I felt when I was on the basketball court. It was a chance to let off some steam. A chance to let out some frustration from our troubled home life.

Playing football was my brothers' chance to be aggressive and not get in trouble for it. It gave him a chance to let all the anger out. He could play aggressively and no one would fault him for it. I was glad he was able to release some frustration from the things we were going through in our personal lives. It was therapy for us.

Watching my brother play brought out different emotions. To see him on that field having fun and breaking records was an amazing feeling. I had my time in the spotlight, but I enjoyed watching my brother even more. It was something he liked doing and he was good at it.

I remember being more nervous for his games than I was for my own games. I just wanted him to do well. I wanted my brother to be happy. I knew playing the sport he loved would provide positive moments in his life.

Taking Charge

George put on a show every Friday, but there were a few games I will never forget. His performances against Pickerington North, Wayne, and Northmont were spectacular! I still can't believe the things my brother did in those games. The way he ran the ball and the way he took the games over was like magic.

In the Pickerington game, George was only a sophomore and he was still playing quarterback. I remember hearing that Pickerington was the sixth ranked team in the Nation! They also had six players who had signed letters of intent to play at Ohio State the following year. To make it tougher they were playing on Pickerington's home field, in front of a sellout crowd. The stakes were really high for this game.

I could tell my brother was pumped up for that game. His performance proved it. He started the game with a lot of energy, and it helped lift his teammates up. They ended up losing the game, but they played them a lot closer than what everyone had expected. George, finished the game with three rushing touchdowns, and two passing touchdowns, along with some spectacular moves. He had an eighty-yard touchdown run in that game that I will never forget. I remember watching him maneuver past eight players then scrambling to score eighty yards later. He wowed the crowd the whole night.

I remember my brother having another stellar performance against Springfield's rival, Wayne. Wayne was a very good team in our conference, and they had beaten Springfield badly during my brothers' sophomore season. They had a chance to redeem themselves at Wayne the following year. And this time they were playing for the conference championship.

The anticipation could not have been any higher. They were conference rivals plus Wayne had beaten them on their home field the year before. It made it even more of a rival considering Wayne's starting quarterback, Braxton Miller had transferred from Springfield to play for Wayne.

I arrived at the game and the stadium was packed! As expected there was nowhere to park and barely any room to sit. I had to find a spot on the sideline to stand, because the crowd was so large. The large crowd brought more intensity from both teams.

You could tell by the way my brother's team was playing that they had wanted revenge for last year's loss. Springfield came out aggressively and went up 21-0 at halftime. My brother scored two of the three touchdowns for his team. Things were looking great in the first half. We were hoping for an easy win, but Wayne stormed back and made it a close contest.

The fourth quarter began and Springfield was still winning by a touchdown 28-21. Wayne had the ball. They drove the ball down the field, and scored with about two minutes left tying the game 28-28. All of the sudden Springfield's momentum was gone and Wayne began to look very confident. Wayne's fans were going berserk while Springfield's fans sat there nervously awaiting the outcome of the game.

It was time for Wayne to kick the ball off to Springfield. I remember telling my friend Isaiah, my brother was going to return the kick and score for us. I really believed he could run the kick back for a touchdown, but I knew it would be tough. Plus, I figured they would kick away from him. But surprisingly they kicked the ball right to him.

Thirty seconds later the ball is in the air and it is coming to the most dangerous player on the field. The crowd was silent as the ball sailed into the air. My brother caught the ball, started running full speed to his right, cut left, jumped between two defenders, and out ran the whole team to score another touchdown!!!

That was his third touchdown of the game! I couldn't believe what I had just watched! Everyone on the Springfield side was going crazy! Screaming, yelling, and jumping around! That touchdown had completely taken the breath out of the Wayne football team.

But George was not finished yet. Plus, Wayne still had enough time to score. And them having Braxton Miller at quarterback made it even more of a possibility to score. Braxton drove his team down the field with ease. It only took three plays to move the ball sixty yards down the field. Wayne was now fifteen yards away from tying the game. The momentum was definitely back on Wayne's side. You could sense the nervousness on the Springfield sideline as they sat quietly waiting to see the outcome.

All it took was a short pass and the game would be tied again. Wayne's fans are now screaming, and yelling, while Springfield's fans are very quiet. They hike the ball, Braxton drops back to pass, throws the ball into the end zone. There is a crowd of players from both teams waiting for the ball. As the ball gets close to the end zone, everyone jumps desperately trying to catch the ball. But somehow MY BROTHER INTERCEPTS THE PASS!!! GAME OVER!

George finished the game with three touchdowns, a kick return that put Springfield ahead, and the game sealing interception! That was the first time Springfield High had ever won the conference championship in football and my brother played a major part in it. I could not have been more proud of my brother.

Brotherly Hug

The Northmont game was the most significant game to me. His performance on the field was incredible, but what he did after the game was even more special. My little brother did something that I will never forget. The whole situation started out in the worst way possible, but he definitely made up for it.

I remember getting a call about my brother getting into a fight with a teammate and hearing he would have to sit the first quarter of the next game. George had played a prank on his teammate and they ended up getting into a fight. So my brother's punishment was to sit the first quarter of the next game. To add to the story line, Northmont was the same team who had given my brother a concussion during his freshman season.

I remember calling my brother all week to get on him for getting into trouble. I was mad at him for getting in trouble in school. He had to have known I was angry because he avoided me the entire week. I had even gone over my mom's house to catch him off guard, but I still could not catch up to him. So I decided to go to the game. I knew he couldn't avoid me there.

The game starts and as expected my brother is on the sideline. Springfield quickly falls behind. It wasn't looking good for them. Northmont was moving the ball very easily. They scored two quick touchdowns, and the Springfield offense looked out of sync without my brother being out there.

The first quarter finally ends and my brother runs out on the field. I could sense he was anxious to play just by the way he ran out there. As soon as they hiked the ball he made an impact. Now Springfield is moving the ball, matching Northmont's intensity. I knew he would come out ferociously, but I could not have predicted the way he would change the game.

George not only brought his team back to win the game, but he finished the game: with three touchdowns, two interceptions, and over two hundred yards rushing! Yet he accumulated those stats after sitting out the first quarter! I was amazed by what I had just watched him do. He displayed total dominance during that game. But again what he did after the game was even more special.

To be honest, my brother had played so well that I had started to look past the incident that happened in school. I was shocked at what I had just seen. The game had ended and I was walking down the bleachers to go home. As I was walking, my brother turned around and asked me to come to the sideline. I could tell my brother knew that I was disappointed by the look on his face. He also knew that I did not approve of him getting in trouble in school. But that wasn't the time or place to discuss that. So, before he could even say anything I told him that he played a hell of a game and that I was proud of him.

What he did next caught me completely off guard. My brother gave me a hug and started crying right there on the sideline! To the average person watching it would have looked like an ordinary hug, but it was so much more than that. That was my brothers' way of telling me that he was sorry for getting in trouble in school. I could tell that he did not want me to be disappointed in him. He didn't have to say it; I knew how he felt by the way he responded. The hug was confirmation.

But those weren't the only reasons the hug was special. It was special because our family rarely ever showed that type of emotion. As mentioned earlier, we were raised in a household where it was easy to show anger, but difficult to express love for one another. Plus, we did not have a father figure to show us how to love one another as brothers. But that moment at the Northmont game was the moment we both needed.

It was difficult to come out and say it, but we both wanted to feel loved. We wanted that type of confirmation from our parents. From our family. But we never received it. However, we learned to express love for each other as brothers. It was something we had taught each other. I wanted to cry with my brother in that moment because it was so special. But I was too embarrassed to really show my emotions in public.

I regretted that, but at the same time I was very, very grateful for that moment. I will never ever forget that hug.

It was just like my brother to initiate a moment like that. Even though I was eight years older, George taught me some things too. That moment really strengthened our bond. I wish someone would have recorded that. It would be great to be able to watch that moment again. It is something I will cherish for the rest of my life.

CHAPTER 16

Weathering the Storm

WITH ALL THE drama taking place in my personal life, it became very easy to get distracted from my goals. Despite those problems I was determined to finish school and get my life back on track. I knew I needed to buckle down and focus on what was important in my life. And at that point, finishing school was the top priority.

After matching up the requirements from Wooster, I enrolled at Clark State to take the classes there. I quickly realized that the Spanish classes were much easier at Clark State than what they were at Wooster. And all I had to do was pass three levels of Spanish to complete the requirements. After that I would be on my way to work as a substitute teacher.

After nine long months of school at Clark State I was finally finished. I earned my Bachelor's degree from the College of Wooster after transferring the credits. I had just become the first person in my entire family to obtain a college degree! It was a rare moment of satisfaction for me. I normally did not give myself credit for the things I had accomplished, but this was different. That situation was special. I had been doubted by many people along the way. I even doubted myself. So to actually earn my degree was a major accomplishment.

After receiving my degree, I thought about the statistics that I heard in class during my freshman year of college. I thought about the stereotypes society put on people like me who grew up in rough neighborhoods. I remembered how certain people looked at me and thought I was just another dumb, black athlete, who couldn't survive in a civilized environment. I remember some of my professors flat out saying they don't give athletes grades because they were good in sports. Those who knew my background didn't give me a fighting chance. But that was fine, I was proud of myself for proving them wrong.

I then went back to that moment during my freshman year of college when I contemplated giving up after hearing those statistics. I felt deeply discouraged after hearing that I had less than a two percent chance of graduating college, because my parents did not graduate high school. It was very disheartening to say the least.

But I dug down and fought through it. It wasn't easy, but I am very thankful that I was able to overcome that. And now that I finished school it was proof that anyone of my siblings could graduate from college too! It was proof that kids in my neighborhood who grew up in the projects, could go to college too! And for once I felt good about myself. I had just accomplished something that I had dreamed of my whole life. And to be honest, I even surprised myself. I thank God for giving me the courage to keep fighting. I could've easily given up after going through so many trials.

Coaching in Springfield

While attending school at Clark State, I received my first coaching assignment at Hayward middle school. The same school I attended ten years earlier. I went into the interview not sure if I was confident enough to coach a team or not. I wasn't sure if I could deal with middle school players and parents. I had only coached during summer camps at Wooster as a volunteer. That was nothing compared to the kids I would deal with at Hayward. Plus, the parents were much more aggressive.

But I didn't have time to question myself. Surprisingly, I was given the job on the spot. There was no way I could back out at that point. If the principal had that much confidence in me I had to go through with it. I figured I would just rely on my experiences as a player to guide me through.

My plan was to teach them to be students first, then incorporate the basics of the game and go from there. I learned so much about character through playing basketball. I wanted to do the same for my players. I wanted to teach the young men everything I learned about life while playing. So I dove in and hoped for the best.

Once the season started, I went back into my pre-game tactics I used as a player. I taught the young men to work hard and to play with discipline. In my mind, that was the best way to coach my players. I walked into an environment where the kids thought they could do whatever they wanted. I had to change that quickly, otherwise the season would've been a disaster.

The parents were even worse. Every parent thought their kid was the best player on the team. Everybody wanted to be the leading scorer. All my players wanted to shoot the ball every time they touched it. I knew that I had to establish roles for each player. Otherwise it would be pure chaos on the court. No one would ever pass the ball. Establishing roles helped me get order on the team.

The parents really began to test me after figuring out I was only twenty-three years old and that was my first coaching job. They thought they could get over on me once they figured that out. It made it even tougher that most of the parents knew me. But I had other plans.

It took some time, but I stuck to my coaching strategy and the parents eventually bought in. Once they realized I was firm in my coaching plan it made things much easier. Everything began to run much smoother that way. I was able to teach the boys more effectively which lead to us developing a bond. The boys noticed that I knew what I was talking about and they began to trust me. Once I earned their trust, we were destined to improve as a team. The boys bought into my system and the team started making strides in a positive direction.

After I had earned the trust of my players I began to enforce other team rules. I created a team behavior sheet for my players. I made it mandatory for everyone on the team to participate in the behavior program. The players were to get the sheet signed by their teachers and turn them in every Friday. The behavior sheet covered class attendance, homework assignments, and overall attitude in the classroom.

I created those sheets because of my experience as a middle school basketball player. I had played at Hayward just ten years before I came back to coach. My team was loaded with talent. In two years of middle school basketball my team did not lose a single game on our home court. And we only lost a total of four games in two years. We scored over eighty points multiple times in just twenty-four minutes of game play. Good was an understatement for our team.

We also made it to the championship game in our eighth-grade season. Our team was so good that coach Park kept fourteen players because it was difficult to make cuts. But here's my point. Out of all that talent, only four of us went on to play in high school. And only two of us played on the collegiate level.

I created those behavior sheets to push my players in the classroom as well as on the court. To prepare those young men for life. To give them a better chance at succeeding at something other than basketball. To create a backup plan to fall back on in case basketball did not work out.

I even took it a step further than that. I started popping up in the classrooms to see what my players were doing. And if they were not behaving in the classroom properly, I made them run extra laps in practice. The parents did not agree with my program, but it wasn't about the parents. I knew from experience that the program would teach the boys discipline that would pay off later in life. I held them accountable for their actions to make them more responsible. If I were a part of something like that it would've changed the way I looked at life.

However, personal conduct wasn't the only issue that came with coaching at Hayward. The boys were not used to winning which affected their attitudes on the court. I asked my players about the teams' previous record. They told me they had won less than five games per season, in the last five years! That was unheard of when I was growing up.

Growing up, Hayward had always dominated all sports in the league. I remember, playing football for Hayward. My team won five games and lost just two. Believe it or not, we were told we had the worst record in the last twenty years! So, to hear that the current team had won less than five games in five years, was a big surprise to me. Especially in basketball!

I was determined to not only prepare these young men for life, but also to bring back a winning attitude. I pushed the boys in practice by teaching them things they had never heard of. They didn't like it at first, but it paid off. Once they noticed how it prepared them for games they were eager to practice harder.

And once we started winning the parents even gave in. My team finished the season with a record of fourteen wins and just five losses in a very tough conference. We also went on to finish third in the league tournament. To make it better, we ended our season by beating our rival, Wayne in the third-place game.

Finishing the season by winning the third-place game was great for the morale of the team. Not only did we receive a medal for winning the game, but we beat a team we had not beaten in years. The future was starting to look very bright. My players had learned what it took to win. The overall confidence of the team had changed. It also helped, that all of my players made major improvements during the season.

After spending so much time with the team, I had become really close with the boys. I stayed in contact with them after the season was over. We eventually started talking about things other than basketball. The boys even started coming to me for personal advice. It was a great feeling to be able to share my personal experiences with the kids I coached. My goal was to tell them what I learned and give them a chance to make better decisions.

We stayed in touch going into the summer. The summers usually consisted of unstructured activities which meant more idle time. The boys normally ran the streets during the summer. But that year I had other plans for them. I had plans to keep them in the gym all summer, off the streets, working on their basketball skills.

It was very difficult to get a gym initially. But I stayed persistent. I knew that if the boys were on the streets too long that they would find trouble. Too much idle time for teenage boys always lead to trouble. If I didn't get them in the gym, I knew they would find something destructive to get in to. So I continued to harass the school officials about getting gym time.

I really started forcing the issue after I received a phone call from a parent. The parent told me that one of my players had come home intoxicated after attending a house party. I couldn't believe what I was hearing. These boys were twelve and thirteen years old!

The next day I went to the school principal and told her about the news I just heard. I also shared my vision of getting the boys off the streets and back on the court. I knew it would make a difference by occupying two hours of their time and putting them in the gym.

As soon as I received permission to use the gym, the summer program took off. The first day of summer open gym I had over thirty boys show up. The next week I had over forty. I remember seeing bikes all over the front of the school. It was a great feeling seeing kids excited to be in the gym. Excited to be a part of something different. I loved seeing the excitement on their faces. It made it even more special knowing the boys were safe.

I also remember seeing the surprised look on Mrs. Samuels (the school principal) face. Her eyes lit up after seeing all of those boys in the gym. That made me feel good. I felt like I was accomplishing something. The excitement coming from the principal confirmed that I was making a positive impact on the kids in the community.

I started open gym by explaining the rules to the boys. I told them that they had to be on time or they would be locked out. There was no jewelry allowed, no arguing, no slap boxing, or horse play allowed. They were in the gym to compete and get better not to play around. Otherwise we would be wasting time.

I created those rules because I felt it would make the boys more aware of their actions. It would also show them how to act in a structured environment. I had always told the boys that when they were on the court, it was business and everyone had a job to do. They could play and be kids after they finished their job. This was my way of preparing the boys for job interviews, college applications, and other serious avenues they would be involved with in the future. They bought into it and we finished the summer on a positive note.

All of my players were very excited coming into the school year. We just finished third in a tough conference, plus my players put in extra work during the summer. There was a small problem though. The system was set up to where the coaches had to stick with a specific grade. Meaning I would have to coach seventh graders the next year while my team went on to the eighth grade. Once I had signed up to coach seventh grade that is where the rules forced me to stay.

But to my surprise, the parents of my seventh-grade team called the school district and insisted that I be allowed to move up with their kids. I couldn't believe what I was hearing. After the rough start with the parents I never imagined them fighting for me to coach their kids the following year. It was a tough task, but I had finally earned the respect of the parents. That was a great feeling considering the crowd I was dealing with.

Last Minute Decision

However, things took another turn. I was offered a job to coach at the high school as the varsity assistant coach for the Springfield High boys team. The change happened suddenly and I was told that I had to take the job immediately. Otherwise I would be left off the high school staff. So I was forced to make a decision quickly. After weighing my options, I decided to take the job at the high school.

The hard part was having to face the boys and tell them the news. I called a meeting and explained to them what was going on. It was very difficult for me to leave so suddenly, but I felt like I had to take the job. I explained to the boys that I would be waiting for them the following year. I also explained that I would come to as many of their games as possible. But they didn't understand. I could tell by the looks on their faces that they weren't happy.

The only reason I agreed to leave was to coach with my best friend, Isaiah Carson had just received the varsity head coaching job. If he had not received the job, I would've stayed one more year to coach my team. Then follow them to high school. The problem is it wouldn't work that way. The high school administrators could not move someone off the high school staff just for me to come and coach.

Still, I felt guilty for leaving the boys at Hayward. I felt like I had let them down by moving up. It didn't help that I received phone calls from some of the parents saying I had abandoned the team. But as I sat and thought about the bigger picture I realized that I would be coaching the boys the following year anyway. It was either leave or stay at the middle school and the boys move up without me. Either way someone would be left behind.

However, there was one particular kid I really had trouble leaving. As a coach, I feel like you shouldn't have favorites. It isn't fair to the other players on the team. But I couldn't help but to love this kid. The boys' name was Stanley.

He, like me did not have a father in his home. He was being raised by a single mother who didn't seem interested in supporting his basketball dreams. I knew what that felt like. I felt empathy for Stanley. But those weren't the only things Stanley and I had in common.

Like me, Stanley was very poor and he was hesitant to ask for help. I remember the other parents putting money together to get him a shirt and tie for the season. We also raised money to get him a decent pair of basketball shoes. Those situations made me feel awful because those were the same exact things that I had gone through as a kid.

After a few incidents I pulled Stanley to the side so none of the other kids would make fun of him. I told him that I would help him as much as I could. I started giving him haircuts. I gave him clothes, hats, and anything else I thought he needed. Some of the same things Coach Parker had done for me when I was in middle school.

At one point, I was seriously considering trying to adopt Stanley. The problem was I was not in a good position to take care of him at that time. So I did the best I could to support him. It really bothered me to see Stanley suffering because I knew exactly how he felt. I knew what it felt like to be ashamed and embarrassed about your living situation.

Stanley was also my favorite because he was the most coach-able kid on the team. Stanley was small and he had to fight for everything he had ever gotten in life. So naturally he was a very scrappy kid. That played into his role for our team. I found a way to add his toughness to our game plan.

I would put Stanley on the opposing teams point guard. He would be all over the kid. I would tell him "Stanley you got the point guard. Don't let him breathe." He would guard that kid full court and completely take him out of his game. It was fun to watch him play defense. Plus, it helped us win games. The other kid would be frustrated in a matter of minutes; dribbling the ball off his leg, throwing the ball all over the place. Which led to easy points for us.

A Bad Move

Moving up to the high school turned out to be a terrible decision. There was trouble before the season had even started. In order to enter the high school building the coaches needed a building code. Otherwise we would have to stand outside the door and wait for someone to let us in.

I was supposed to get a building code along with keys to the locker room the first day I signed the contract. But for some reason it took the athletic director, Michael Staley three months to give me the code and the keys. So for three months I had to use a code given to me from another coach just to enter the building.

I had heard stories about how difficult it was to work with Staley, but I had never dealt with him on a personal level. So I didn't know how true the allegations were. However, I would soon find out that Staley was a nightmare to work with. Instead of working with us he did whatever he could to make things difficult. It seemed like he was there to cause trouble.

My one-year coaching at Springfield High turned out to be the worst basketball season I had ever had as a coach or as a player. Dealing with Staley and Wilma Frank were enough to make anyone not want to coach anymore. Wilma Frank worked on the school board. Her husband used to coach so she was always snooping around with Staley.

To make things worse, we had a horrible season. We only won six games that year. We lost our best player Rick Manning for over fifteen games after an illegal interrogation by Staley. Then we lost our leading scorer, Brandon Darby for five games after a silly incident in the cafeteria. The season was a complete disaster. I had never lost that many games in one season in my entire career!

Once the season ended I did not go back to coaching for multiple reasons. And even though things did not go as planned it was great to be able to coach alongside my best friend Isaiah. I wish them nothing but success as I still support the Wildcats today. The timing was just off with that situation.

Giving Professional Basketball, Another Try

After I finished coaching, I figured I would get out of Springfield and go back to playing professional basketball. The only reason I was in Springfield was to be involved in my daughter's life, but I was only seeing her once a week. I figured I would go play for a year, save the money up and hire a better attorney to get more rights to my daughter. Staying in Springfield wasn't doing anything for me. Plus, there weren't any good paying jobs in Springfield.

I got in touch with one of my previous agents, to see if she knew of any teams who needed an American guard. She quickly found an open tryout for a league in Japan. She advised me that I would be trying out with local, first year players. The scouts were going to be present during the tryout and they were signing players on the spot. She also told me that the pay range was $40,000 to $80,000 depending on how well I performed. After hearing the details, I started working out again.

I was set to fly from Columbus to Detroit then to Japan. The trip started off rough and ended in a disaster. The flight from Columbus was a little behind so I literally ran through the entire Detroit airport trying to make it to the gate on time. When I finally arrived at the gate the attendant advised me that the flight had already left! As soon as I heard the news I went into panic mode!

Not only did I just miss the flight, but I was also stranded in Detroit. Now I had to find a way back home and I most likely missed out on a great opportunity. I then contacted my agent through email and let her know what happened. She told me she would talk to the league president and set it up for the following day.

Luckily for me, the airline agreed to reimburse everyone who missed their flight to Japan and the president of the league agreed to allow me to tryout the following day. I arrived to the airport the next day to a gate full of frustrated people. I was one of only four Americans waiting to board the plane. I began to feel out of place again the way I did in

Germany. Hearing hundreds of people speaking, but not understanding a single word they were saying.

However, that would be the least of my problems. Entry to the plane kept being delayed because of mechanical problems. The delay would eventually last for more than an hour. After running out of excuses, the flight attendant finally told us the truth. The flight was to be canceled because of a gas leak. It obviously wasn't safe to fly under those conditions.

They offered everyone another free night in the hotel, but I was frustrated and ready to go home. I had sat in the hotel room bored one night, I wasn't going to do it again. To make matters worse, the president of the league in Japan could not post pone the tryout another day. So not only did I miss a flight and get stuck in Detroit, but I missed the whole tryout.

Three months later, I realized that it was not God's plan for me to play basketball in Japan. A couple months after I was supposed to be in Japan they had a typhoon that wiped out an entire city. I watched the whole thing on the news back home in Springfield. I could not believe what I was watching. I could not imagine how I would have felt to actually be living there going through something like that.

After the Japan tryout fell through I decided I would give professional basketball one last try. I signed up for a combine in South Carolina. The guys who ran the combine claimed to have connects to teams overseas. I was trying to force myself to get back into it. But once I participated in the combine I realized that I no longer had the passion for it anymore.

I had grown tired of the extreme workouts. Tired of the pressure, the grind, the constant traveling, and extra stuff that came with playing basketball. It was also a lot of work trying to learn the culture of the country I would be living in. After the last disappointment I felt God was telling me that he had other plans for me.

Introducing Mr. Cooper

Not long after deciding to pursue a career other than basketball, I moved out of my father's house and started rooming with my long-time friend, Kyle Wheeler. It was the beginning to a better, brighter future. After the move I finished my classes at Clark State. I received my Bachelor's degree and I received my first assignment as a substitute teacher.

I was overwhelmed with joy and excitement about working as a teacher. I never imagined myself working that profession. At the same time, I was honored about the opportunity. I was honored that the school district thought I was good enough to be a teacher. I felt like I accomplished something special.

For a while I had felt good about myself. I had set out to finish school, so that I could get a better job and I accomplished that. How many people could say they lived in every project housing facility in Springfield then went on to become a teacher? I could and it made me proud to be in that position.

Going Nowhere Fast

I had made some improvements in my personal life, but I still had a long way to go. I had to continue to get better in order to reach my goals and become the person I wanted to be. I had just started drinking at the age of twenty-four, and I quickly became addicted to the party life. Me and a group of friends would go out every weekend on Fridays, and Saturdays. We started going out locally, but that became boring after a while so we branched out to Dayton and Columbus. Club hopping was something I had never experienced before. But even though I started late I quickly grew tired of it.

I felt like the club life was not meant for me. So I started looking for a reason to get away from it. This is around the time I met the woman I would marry. But because of my mindset of trying to find a reason to change I made a horrible decision. Truth be told I married her because of the idea of marriage. In my mind, that was what responsible people did. Me marrying her had nothing to do with her personality or our chemistry. And it showed. The marriage ended in just six months.

CHAPTER 17

Worst Day of My Life

I GREW UP in a hostile environment to say the least. There were a lot of things that happened in my life that weren't normal. The drama, the hurt, pain and frustration never seemed to go away. But in my twenty-eight years on earth nothing could compare to the day I lost my brother. I never thought a person could feel so much pain and survive. There were many moments I experienced where I really thought my heart would stop.

It was Friday, May 30, 2014. I remember it like it was yesterday. I had woken up around 8:30 am and it seemed like it was going to be a typical day. The sun was shining and the weather was great as I was driving to Springfield from Fairborn. I had spoken to my little brother the day before about working out with him.

I was helping him get in shape for his upcoming football season at Georgia Military school. He had been home for a couple months after a short stint at Walsh University. He was having a difficult time getting comfortable, so he decided to transfer to another school. I agreed to help him get in shape because I wanted him to get away from Springfield as soon as possible.

My brother was having a hard time adjusting to the college life (which most freshman do) and he wanted to come home. I knew from experience that the first semester would be very difficult. That first semester was tough for me too, but I knew that once he had gotten through that initial stage, he would be fine.

With my brother being the youngest, my mom tried to do everything for him. I understood my mom's perspective of protecting her son. At the same time, encouraging him to come home would only hurt him in the long run. There was nothing for him, but trouble in Springfield. Staying in school would've definitely been the best option for my brother.

Me and my mom got into a heated argument when my brother had first come home from school. I couldn't believe she had encouraged him to come home! There was nothing positive for him to do in Springfield. There were barely any jobs and there wasn't much to do besides hang out at the local bars. And I was already seeing his friends sitting around smoking and drinking every day.

I didn't want my brother to waste his life coming back to Springfield. Plus, the crime rate had gone up tremendously. Guns were more accessible than they had ever been before. Things were really beginning to get rough in our city. So I definitely didn't want my brother living there.

Other young men his age where forming small gangs, breaking in houses, shooting, and robbing each other. Just a bunch of non-sense. I feared my brother would get caught up in that lifestyle and get himself in trouble. So I made sure we stayed in contact with each other on a daily basis. My goal was to keep his mind occupied on getting out of Springfield.

My plan had worked. After just two months of being home my brother was starting to see what I was seeing. He began calling me telling me how he missed school. He couldn't find a job in Springfield; all his friends were still sitting around doing nothing, and there was no one there to push him. The minute he told me he was serious about getting back out of Springfield we started working out.

First Sign of Trouble

My brother had gotten extra motivation after a tragic situation occurred. A local football star, Jeff Wellington had gotten shot and killed in Springfield the night before Easter. Jeff was shot by a classmate while trying to break up a fight. He was only eighteen years old when he was murdered. Jeff and my brother knew each other through mutual friends. They even wore the same number on the football field. That situation really scared my brother.

I had coached Jeff when he was playing basketball in middle school. Jeff was the type of kid that everyone loved to be around. He was always laughing, cracking jokes, singing, and being silly. When I first heard the news I was shocked. I couldn't imagine anyone wanting to purposely hurt Jeff. It just didn't make sense to me. Jeff was by far the silliest kid I had ever coached. He was full of positive energy.

After Jeff was shot it really woke Little George up. He was more motivated than ever to get back on the football field and away from the trouble in Springfield. My brother then reached out to his father to pick him up to go stay with him in Dayton. He had planned on staying with his father until it was time to leave for school. But his dad never came. He always had an excuse for why he couldn't pick my brother up. But I figured I would step in and help my brother stay motivated.

On that day, May 30, 2014, I called my brother and told him I would be in Springfield around 9:00 am. The plan was to pick him up from mom's and go workout at Hayward. I arrived in Springfield around that time and I drove past my mom's house, but he wasn't on the porch. As I was driving past my mom's house I called my brother to see where he was at. He told me he was at Drew's house and he was walking to Grand. I figured I would just pick him up from there then head to the track to workout.

Before I went to pick my brother up I stopped by Clark State Community College, to talk to their basketball coach about using the gym. I had just walked up to coach and after I said about two words my phone went off but I ignored the call. Right after the call I received an inbox from my cousin on Facebook. I glanced at the message and returned to my conversation. But after talking for a minute I realized what the message had said. The message said, "YOUR BROTHER GOT SHOT IN THE FACE!"

Once I was able to fully comprehend what the message was saying I panicked. I started jogging to my car trying to understand what I had just read. For some reason my mind was numb. I wasn't sprinting yet because I was already in shock after reading that message. I knew what I read, but my mind had not fully processed it yet.

I finally reach the car and as soon as I closed the door my phone starts going off like crazy. I get a call from a name I don't recognize. I answer the call and the girl just starts talking not making any sense. She said, "I can't believe they shot that baby" and she keeps repeating herself. I ask who it was, but she just keeps saying the same thing. So I get annoyed and hang up. The girl on the phone calls right back, but this time she is crying and screaming, "somebody shot that baby, somebody shot him."

By this time, I am driving recklessly to the hospital, flying past cars, refusing to stop for traffic lights or stop signs. I call my best friend Isaiah Carson and I tell him that somebody shot my brother. I remember telling him that whoever shot my brother better hope he makes it. They better hope he doesn't die.

As soon as I hang up I get a call from the girl again. By this time, I am parked in front of the hospital. She is even worse than earlier. She screams into the phone "he didn't make it! He didn't make it. He died!" That is when I finally realized that the girl calling me was my sister Heather! I instantly lost all composure. I remember parking my car, getting out, and punching the hood repeatedly! I then started to yell in disbelief! I couldn't believe what I had just heard! There's no way this can be true!

Parked right beside me was my brothers' aunt, and his first cousins. I got out the car and everyone began to yell! I remember Saalim, my brothers' cousin saying, "it was Dennis. Dennis did it."

I still couldn't believe what was going on. I had just talked to my brother! There's no way this can be true! No way! I was supposed to be picking him up, going to work out. I had spoken with my brother at exactly 9:59 am and he was pronounced dead at 10:23 am. Just twenty-four minutes after we hung the phone up! I couldn't wrap my head around what I had just heard. My mind was completely fried.

The thought of me talking to my brother so close to his death was starting to drive me crazy. I blamed myself. I asked myself why I didn't go straight to Grand instead of going to Clark State first? Who would shoot my brother and why? I was angry, I was hurt, I was confused. I had a billion thoughts going through my head at once. My head felt like

I was spinning in circles. I began to feel a pain I had never felt before.

I still couldn't believe what I had just heard! I needed proof! I wanted to see! What about mom? How is she going to react? I just talked to him! Wait! He is my only brother! He is supposed to be going to college! I planned on watching him play in the NFL one day! This has to be a mix up! Is it really him? This has to be a mistaken identity! All of these thoughts were running through my head at once.

I knew I had to call my mom. I was scared before I even made the phone call because I knew it would crush her. To make it worse, she was at work. I called her and it went exactly the way I thought it would. As soon as I told her she went crazy. It made me feel even worse. The whole conversation was terrible. As soon as she answered the phone I yelled, "HE'S FUCKIN DEAD MOM! HE DIED!" At that point I had no control over my emotions. I had completely lost all composure. I was devastated! I was hurt beyond words! Who would ever think that one day someone would shoot my brother?!

After I hung the phone up from calling my mom I slowly turn around and noticed the hospital parking lot was crowded. I was so distraught that I had not seen or heard anyone pull up. My mind was on another planet. In a matter of minutes there were crowds of people screaming in front of the hospital building. You could hear the pain in everyone's voices. We all stood and cried in disbelief. He was just with us and now he is gone.

Not long after, my mom came flying into the parking lot. As soon as she pulled up she got out of the car and fell to the ground. I remember picking her up and walking into the hospital emergency room. I don't even remember who moved her car. But I knew that I could not allow her to lay on the ground like that.

Even though all of that was going on, I still could not process what I had heard. We needed answers. I needed to know if he was really gone. I refused to believe it. We walked up to the receptionist to see what was going on. We were confused because some people were saying he was care flighted and some were saying he passed away. So I nervously walked up to the receptionist and asked about my brother. With no emotion, she told me that he had passed a while ago. Hearing that struck lighting through my body. My heart, head, even my legs started to hurt. I knew I had to sit down before I passed out. It made that nightmare a reality. Before she confirmed it I desperately hoped and prayed that it was a mix up. I hoped this was just another one of his jokes. But unfortunately it wasn't.

The news was so bad that it made it difficult for me to move. It was hard to breathe. I couldn't think. I felt like my head was going to spin off. We ended up staying at the hospital for over an hour still in shock. Majority of our family was still scattered all through the parking lot and the waiting room. It had gotten so crowded that the security in the hospital had to force everyone to leave.

My mind was so far gone that I don't even remember driving to my mom's house after we left the hospital. I don't remember walking to my car. I don't remember starting my car. I just remember sitting in her front room in an awkward silence. Everyone was quiet. No one said a word. We all just continued to cry. At that point, I had already cried so much that my eyes were swollen and my head hurt. The pain was unbearable. But sadly, that was only the beginning of what was to come.

For the next six months I fell into a deep depression. I couldn't sleep more than two hours a night. I didn't have an appetite. I had to force myself to eat and even after forcing myself, I only ate once a day. I was hurt beyond words. I couldn't believe someone had the nerve to shoot my brother. My only brother!

Everything I had gone through was nothing compared to this feeling. No pain could be worse than the pain I had felt at that time. I wanted to die. For months, I asked God to take me away. I couldn't deal with so much pain every minute of every day. I just couldn't do it. I literally thought about my brother every hour of every day. Then, when I was finally able to sleep for an hour or two, I had dreams about him. I was going crazy. I had completely lost my mind. I cried for months! I isolated myself from everyone. I felt like nothing could help me. I didn't think I would ever get over it.

Reality Sinks In

Sunday June 1, 2014, me and my family met with the directors of the funeral home to create the funeral arrangements. The whole scene was absolutely terrible! It was one of the most difficult things I have ever had to do in my life. We were planning a funeral for the baby of the family. Wow!

Even though I didn't want to, I had to communicate with the funeral director. My mom was too distraught to talk. And believe it or not, all my step-grandma was worried about was which side of the family was mentioned more in the obituary. I was ready to snap and hurt everyone in the room. I could not believe how she was acting! At the worst possible time!

But despite the ignorance I had to block her out and plan my baby brother's funeral. I had to be strong. I had to make sure the arrangements were set. It hurt very, very badly though. Looking back, I don't know how I got through that situation. It was the toughest thing I have ever had to do.

I stumbled through the whole process. I couldn't stop thinking about my brother and what happened to him. But I forced my way through the hurt feelings. I just tried to do it as quickly as possible. I picked out the casket. Then I had to choose the time and place of the funeral. I prayed to God silently throughout the whole process. I asked God for guidance. I asked Him for strength to keep going. There's no way I got through that on my own.

Once the arrangements were finished the funeral director asked if we had any more questions. My mom spoke up and said she wanted to view my brother's body. The funeral director (with a very surprised look on her face) asked why we had not identified his body at the hospital. My mom informed her that the police would not allow her to see him, stating it was an open investigation.

The funeral director told my mom that they normally did not allow families to see the body of the deceased person, until the funeral. Still, my mom insisted on seeing my brother, so the director agreed to let her see him. But she warned my mom that they had not cleaned him up yet. She then asked if my mom was sure she still wanted to see him in that condition.

Just the thought of seeing my brother dead brought extreme stress!

I immediately leaned over and tried to persuade my mom to wait until the funeral. But she insisted on seeing him. My heart instantly dropped. I was so scared that I started shaking. The thought of seeing my brother like that scared the life out of me. I knew it was going to be a horrible scene!

Initially I told my mom that I was not going in there. I knew I would not be able to bare seeing him like that. But once my mom went into the room and I heard her screams, I felt like I had to go in to help. I opened the door and before I could walk in I seen my brothers body and I froze! I could not move. My mind and my body had stopped working. It was the worst thing I had ever seen in my entire life! God it hurt so bad!!! There he was. My baby brother laying there lifeless! I wanted to die right there. Every part of me wanted to leave this earth. I couldn't take it. It took the breath completely out of my body.

This is the same little boy I shared so much with growing up. My only brother! The same boy who followed me around. The same baby we all waited anxiously to meet. After having five girls in a row my mom finally had a boy. I was so excited to have a baby brother. And to see him laying not able to talk or move was enough to take me under.

The first thing I noticed was the platform holding his head up. It made my heart hurt. Literally. I could feel the pain running through my body. I felt like a was paralyzed. I didn't know how I was standing up. I couldn't feel anything. Just extreme pressure in my chest and in my head. I couldn't talk or move. I just stood there with tears running down my face.

After standing in the doorway for what seemed like hours, I was finally able to walk up to my brother. The feelings in my chest started to get worse as I looked at the blood splatter in his hair. After seeing the blood splatter, a shocking image flashed in my mind of my brother being shot. Everything in my body began to ache. I started to lose my mind right there. I had never in my life felt so much anger and hurt at the same time. It was very difficult to face the reality that my brother was really gone. I stared at his face desperately wishing he could get up and walk away. I wished it was one of his pranks. I would've done anything to bring him back.

But those thoughts were overshadowed by me visualizing the bullet going through my brother's body; the thought of my brother taking his last breath. I just knew in my mind that my brother was calling for me. I felt like shit because I wasn't there. That was my job. To protect my brother, but I failed. How could let my baby brother get shot? Why I am still alive at twenty-eight, but my brother only lived to see twenty? It wasn't fair! Those thoughts continued to run through my mind. I couldn't shake them. I continued to battle those thoughts every day for the next two years. It began to control my mind.

After six months of refusing to believe what had happened to my brother I began to try to deal with his loss. I played the situation in my head over and over. Trying to figure out what really took place that day. I remember my brother telling me he was at Drew's house on Southern. Which was right around the corner from Marcus' house on Grand. (where he was shot) I envisioned him walking to Marcus' house and the path he took. But from there I couldn't figure out what had happened. It didn't help that I had heard ten different stories about what happened to my brother.

Imagine losing your only brother in a matter of minutes then hearing people talk about his death like it was after school gossip. Everybody wanted to have a part in the story. I heard so many stories. So many different scenarios. It was really driving me crazy. It was bad enough that I was the last person to talk to him. Now I have to hear about his death every day?

The different stories only made me feel worse. I couldn't help, but think how things would've been different if I had just pulled up earlier. I could've saved him. I would've taken the bullet for him.

The stories literally broke me down. Every time I heard a different story I replayed the situation in my head. I had heard that my brother was shot six times. Then I heard he was shot four times. I heard he was shot in his face. I heard he was shot in his chest. I heard he was pushed into the bullet. I had heard so many stories that it was making me think I was losing my mind. I didn't know what to believe. I didn't know who to trust. I kept reliving the moment. I kept imagining the bullets penetrating my brother's skin. My heart hurt just thinking about it.

I began to drown in pain. It had gotten so bad that I had to be intoxicated to be able to sleep. Otherwise I would be up all night thinking a million thoughts about what happened to my brother. I would cry. I would break out in sweats. I would experience bursts of angry frustration. I just couldn't stop thinking about that situation. So I began to drink myself to sleep to avoid dealing with the reality that my brother was gone.

After a while, the drinking became ineffective. So I had find another way to deal with the pain. One night I sat up thinking for hours how I was going to find out who killed my brother. I was determined to pay them back for what they had done. I wanted to get vengeance in any way I could get it. I didn't care how I did it. I just wanted the people responsible to pay for harming my brother.

My family and those around me were thinking the same. My older cousin had given me a gun for both protection, and a way to get vengeance on those responsible. I kept the gun for a couple days, but I had to return it. Even though I was hurt out of my mind I still had enough sense to know that carrying a gun would only lead to more trouble.

Plus, carrying a gun wasn't for me. I had never carried a gun in my life. I felt uncomfortable even touching it. I had always thought guns were for cowards. I also knew that I could not allow other people's actions to change the person I was, or what I stood for. And even though I was crushed, I would much rather fight using my hands, than to use a gun any day.

I wasn't the only one in my family suffering though. Nobody understood what we were dealing with. A death can ruin a family. Especially a sudden death involving the youngest child. He had so much to live for. He was supposed to be playing football in Georgia. Away from Springfield. Living a good life. Then in a matter of seconds he is gone. That right there is enough to make a person go crazy.

My mom felt the pain a lot more than my sisters did though. I honestly felt that a lot of things were said in public for attention. But behind closed doors their actions did not come close to matching the things they were saying in front of people. My mom on the other hand was really going through some tough times.

I could see it in her face and in her actions. I remember my mom calling me asking me to stay with her at her house. When I arrived at my mom's it bothered me to see that all the lights in the house were on. I then realized that the death of my brother had caused my mom to be afraid of the dark. I could relate because I, myself began to experience things that I had never experienced before.

After George's death, I began to experience severe anxiety. Then I became claustrophobic all of the sudden. At times I would be thinking about what happened and my heart would start beating extremely fast. Once it started it took a while to slow down. It was a scary feeling. When I had seen that my mom had every light in the house turned on, I realized that she was experiencing some of the same things that I was dealing with.

Seeing my mom become afraid of the dark bothered me. It was even worse seeing her cry every day. This went on for months. That was the worst feeling because I didn't know how to help. I was feeling just as much pain myself, so how could I help her? There were days where we just sat in the house and cried for hours.

The days leading up to the funeral were long. They were dreadful. I was scared because I knew I would have to see my brother lay in a casket. I was scared because I knew he would look different. I didn't want to see him like that. I knew that seeing him in the casket would make the whole situation a reality. That he was really was gone forever and there was nothing I could do to bring him back. It was a terrible, dreadful feeling.

I remember us sitting in my moms' front room trying to figure out what my brother was going to wear for the funeral. The whole discussion bothered me from the start. I couldn't believe we were sitting in a room discussing what my twenty-year old brother was going to wear to his funeral! It bothered me even more how playful my sister was about the whole situation. I couldn't take it. The thought of putting the clothes on his limp body bothered me so much that I broke down in tears. I had to leave the house. I couldn't deal with it.

Discussing the clothes he would wear was not the only thing that bothered me. Every time I heard an ambulance siren go off I instantly broke down in tears. It made me think of my brother riding in the ambulance on his way to the hospital, the day he was shot. The smallest things began to bother me. Everything seemed to remind me of my brother.

I was severely depressed, but I had no idea of how to deal with it. The pain would not go away. No matter how much I prayed or begged God to take it away. And for the first time in my life, I didn't have any control over my emotions. I was used to holding things in and acting as if everything was okay. But this situation was too much for me to deal with alone. I needed God. I had to find a way to get closer to God. I knew that was the only way I would get through that situation alive.

Disbelief

After we had planned the funeral it was time to find a location. My brother had gotten baptized at a local church, so we figured we would have the funeral there. To our surprise, the Pastor of the church rejected us! I couldn't believe what I was hearing. The church where my brother was baptized just turned us away from having his funeral there. I was so surprised that I didn't know how to react.

Things continued to get worse though. The same Pastor who had denied us to hold the funeral at his church, held a peace walk for my brother the following day. Once he had figured out how popular George was, he decided to have a peace walk to get clout for his church.

Even after he just denied us for the funeral service! Not only did he have the peace walk, but he held the event without consulting anyone in our family. I'm not even going to say what my thoughts were at the time. Anger is an understatement for how I was feeling. But we eventually worked it out. Saint Johns' Pastor, Ernest Brown allowed us to have the services there.

Dying a Second Time

I don't remember sleeping during the week leading up to the funeral. I didn't like funerals to begin with, so I definitely wasn't ready to attend a funeral for my own brother. I felt emotions I had never felt the morning of the funeral. When I had first walked outside I remember looking up and not seeing a cloud in the sky. The weather was nearly perfect, yet I felt awful. All I could think about was how scared I was going to be walking up to my brother's casket. I didn't know how I was going to react.

I remember everyone getting up to get dressed in silence that morning. No one said a word. You could sense something was wrong because everyone in the house was silent. You could hear a pin drop it was so quiet in the house that morning. We were all trying to come to terms with the loss of the baby of the family.

Not long after getting ready, I remember people showing up at my mom's house. Family we had not seen in years had gathered in the front of the house to pray. That was very irritating. I was annoyed because we had not seen these people in years even though we lived in the same city. It was like an event for them. They weren't there because they cared about my brother. They were there for show. I guess they all wanted to be a part of the event. Pretend like we were a loving family.

I was even more annoyed that my step father was nowhere to be found. He was supposed to ride with us to the funeral. I couldn't believe he was late. We waited around until it was almost time for the funeral to start. We had to leave, otherwise we would've been late. I was so angry that I had actually thought about attacking my step-father when I saw him. How could he not show up and ride with the rest of the family?! I felt like that was very disrespectful to my brother.

We finally arrive to the church and I can't believe what I was seeing. We are greeted by a crowd so large that it circled around the block. It was pandemonium outside. There were cars everywhere. People all over the street. I couldn't believe how many people were there. People crowded the block wearing shirts in remembrance of my brother.

However, the quietness made it awkward. To see that many people and it be that quiet felt weird. You could sense the tension in the air. But I had to focus on being strong for my brother. As I got out the car to walk into the church, each step I took made me more afraid. There was no way I would ever not show up to pay respect to my baby brother, but it was very difficult to see him like that. The whole time I was walking I thought about turning around and not going into the church.

I don't know why, but I was the first person to walk into the church.

I remember feeling like my body was floating. I could not feel my legs moving at all. It was a weird feeling. It felt like I was having an outer body experience. Something I had never felt before. The whole situation was a nightmare.

When I finally reached my brother I just stood there. I felt like it was just me and him. I had completely locked in on my brother. I examined his face first. I looked at his facial hair and his haircut. I was afraid to touch him. My heart was pounding. I was dying inside. I wanted to be with my brother. I wished I could wake him up. The thought of this being the last time I would see him in the flesh, started to run through my mind. The feeling of being paralyzed came back. I could not move away from my brother. So I just stood there staring at him.

After standing over my brother for a couple minutes, I finally found the strength to touch him. I felt his face and I remember touching his arm after I touched his face. When I touched him it felt like lightning had struck through my entire body. My heart began to ache. I felt the anxiety taking over my mind. But for some reason I couldn't cry. I felt like I couldn't use my voice. I remember his arm being extremely hard. It felt fake. I began to think to myself, "this isn't my brother. This isn't real." I wouldn't believe it. I just couldn't.

He looked so calm laying there. It just didn't seem like him. He was usually laughing whenever we were around each other. He was always full of energy. This time he looked like he was in a calm state of mind. Still, I wanted him back. I started thinking about us as kids. I thought about the chubby little kid who followed me around.

The same little boy who wanted to go everywhere I went. And if I didn't let him he would cry and tell mom. The same kid who wanted to watch scary movies, then cry at night because he was afraid. I remember he used to have a VHS tape in his hand waiting for me to come home and play it for him. I would have done anything to have one of those moments back. My heart began to melt. My body began to shake. This couldn't be real. I refused to leave my brothers side. I had never felt pain that ran so deep. I didn't know how to deal with it.

The funeral workers were beginning to get frustrated because I was holding the line up. They asked me to move, but I refused. I had been standing in the front of the church forcing everyone to walk around me. But I didn't care! That was my brother and that would be the last time I would see him! I didn't care about anyone else! And if anyone would've said anything I would've snapped!

I remember noticing how crowded the church was when I finally sat down. The visitors crowded the church and spilled out into the street. They finally closed the doors to start the funeral. Then the pastors began to preach about my brother. Reverend Michael Cooper spoke last. He finished his sermon by asking if anyone had anything to say on my brother's behalf.

He then volunteered for me to say a few words. I was nervous and I was not in the mood to talk, but I had to say something for my brother. In my mind I was doing this for Little George. Pastor Cooper actually did me a favor. If he had not called me up there I probably would not have gotten on the stage to talk. And if I had not said anything I would've regretted that for the rest of my life. With him calling me out, I felt like I had to get up there and say something.

Once I had gotten up there my head started spinning. I was trying to work through the pain and speak for my brother. But it was very difficult to try to speak in a normal tone. My voice trembled during the entire speech. I fought tears the whole time I was on the stage. My mind told me to break down, but I had to hold it together for my brother. It was his time it wasn't about me.

I began to speak about the first thing that came to my mind. That was, the extraordinary person George Walker Jr. was. I spoke about my brother as a child. I spoke about him on the football field. I spoke about the impact he had on our family. How he was always being silly, making everyone laugh. How we used to watch him play with his nieces and nephews.

Once the funeral was over we headed to the cemetery for the burial. I remember being followed by a crowd of cars. My brother's funeral was so large that the police had to stop traffic in advance to avoid an accident from happening. I had never witnessed a funeral so large in person. It looked like a funeral capacity for a celebrity. Something you would see on television. Seeing so many people show support for my brother felt good for a moment, but it wasn't enough to overshadow the pain of losing him.

After the burial we met at my mom's house. Family, friends, and associates were meeting there to eat and celebrate my brother's life. I wasn't in the mood, but I had to hold it together for my family. I was hurting, but I had to make sure nothing went wrong. After getting to moms, and getting settled in, I noticed that my step dad was nowhere to be found. Everyone in our family was present except for him.

I later found out that he had taken his other son to play in a basketball game! So not only did he arrive to the funeral late, but he also left early to go to a basketball game! I felt like my step-father had totally disrespected my brother. I was furious after discovering that information. But again I had to put it aside for the time being. The last thing we needed was more drama.

So I told myself that I would deal with my step-father later. I knew that if I had gone off and lost composure it would've turned into a disaster. Everything would've gotten out of control quickly. And with the tension already being so high, anything was liable to happen. So I kept it to myself and acted as if everything was okay.

Mom's house stayed crowded for hours. We had family and friends in the house, on the front porch, and even on the side of the house. But after a while my mom wanted to be alone. Seeing people all day after attending my brothers' funeral was draining. So I asked everyone to leave the house so my mom could rest.

Once everybody left, the house instantly became quiet again. And when it was quiet all those horrible feelings came rushing back. Reality hit me once again. My brother was really gone. I was somehow able to keep my mind occupied while people were in front of me, but that idle time was the worst! All the crazy thoughts began to come back to me. I wanted to break down and cry, but I couldn't, I was too weak. I didn't have any tears left after crying for a week straight.

Other Factors That Made it Difficult to Deal with My Brother's Death

I felt like my brother did not get a chance to live his life. He did not get a chance to make his own decisions as a man. That bothered me severely because our childhood was horrible. As kids we didn't have a fighting chance. There was always something going on. Plus, I knew from experience how going to college, and being surrounded by positive people changed my whole perspective on life.

I wanted my brother to get a chance to experience that. Be surrounded by people who wanted to see him make it. A chance to live in a better environment than what we had grown up in. But he didn't get a chance to do that. Most of his decisions were dictated by his parents. And that bothers me because we will never know what kind of person he would've turned out to be. We are left with pictures, memories, and hundreds of questions about the person he could have been.

How My Brother's Death Affected My Mom

We had thought the funeral was going to be the worst of it, but we were wrong. Dealing with the loss of my brother became worse as more time passed by. Each day of him being away made it clear that he was not coming back. And it hurt more each day waking up realizing what had happened to my brother.

I later noticed that my mom was reluctant to leave her house. And as I started paying more attention I noticed that she was not leaving her house at all. She stayed in the house for months, following my brother's death. She didn't go to the store, to put gas in her car or anything. My mom was going through a very tough time. Then her job (which she worked for over five years) let her go for missing too many days. Not showing any sympathy for the fact that she had just lost her youngest son.

I remember sitting and thinking of ways to get my mom to leave the house. I knew it was hard for her to want to leave. I knew from experience how it felt to want to be alone. Wanting to exclude yourself from everyone to sit in a dark room. But I also learned that sitting alone only made it worse. After a while you would feel stuck, trapped in that mindset. And you would dwell on the situation the whole day.

After nearly three months of my mom sitting in the house, I had come up with an idea to get her out. My mom's birthday was coming up, so I figured I would put together a surprise party. That would draw her out of the house. I called every one of my mom's friends, and all of our family. I told them that she needed them to be there for support. The list quickly grew to more than a hundred people.

I knew that if I had told her I was having a party for her, that she wouldn't come. So I had to make up a story to get her out of the house. My older cousin, Danielle worked as a bartender at Strivers; so I told my mom that I had to run in and grab something from her. I then told my mom to come in with me. But I had her walk in first.

Everyone was inside waiting, with their cameras, and camera phones ready. When she walked in she was welcomed with a loud yell of "surprise" by all of her friends and family! She was completely caught off guard. It even brought tears of joy to my mom's eyes. The surprise had turned out perfectly!

My mom ended up having the time of her life. I'm happy I put that party together. And even though it was only one night. It was one night where everyone in my family had gotten along. No drama, no arguments, just smiles. I even heard laughter from my mom and my sisters for the first time in a while. To make it better, it was on my mom's birthday. I'm sure she will never forget that night.

Trying to Live After the Loss of My Brother

After losing my brother I lost control of everything. I could barely function. All I could think about was my brother being murdered. It began to take over my mind. It caused me to isolate myself from everyone. I spent a lot of time alone because I had gotten tired of people being in my face. Asking me questions about what happened. I also didn't like crying in front of people. It felt weird to me. I felt weak when I had cried. And I felt weaker when other people seen me cry.

Friends and family kept telling me to try grief therapy. But I refused to try it. I already knew what the therapists were going to say. I knew what they were going to ask me. I felt like they couldn't help me. I also didn't trust anyone to share that type of information with.

But one Sunday afternoon would change my outlook on trying counseling. I was staying with my friend, Isaiah Carson at the time. After another night of not sleeping, crying all day, I decided I would stay in my room and try to sleep. I felt like a zombie. My eyes were swollen. I didn't have any energy. I just wanted to sleep. I remember desperately praying for God to allow me to sleep. I was desperate for rest, but my mind would not allow me to. I couldn't stop thinking about my brother.

So I sat there and stared at the wall for over eight hours straight. At that moment I knew I had to get some professional help. I had to put my pride aside and ask for help. I had to try to trust someone. I felt that if I didn't get help I was going to have a mental breakdown. That was not a normal way to try to function. So the next day I went to a grief counselor to get help.

And as expected, I didn't like the grief therapy. I didn't like it because he asked the questions I had anticipated he would ask. And instead of helping it made me angry. So I decided to try counseling with my cousin, Willie White. That was much more helpful than the grief therapy. I felt like my cousin understood some of the things I was feeling. It also helped that he was a spiritual counselor. He was able to counsel me while also teaching me how to depend on God. That made a lot of sense to me. It helped me deal with my brother's loss in a better way.

My cousin Willie wasn't my only counselor though. I reached out to other Pastors I had known and asked for help. Not because I wasn't satisfied with Willie, but to get different perspectives. I also felt like I was complaining after talking to one person repeatedly about my problems. I had developed this complex of not wanting to hear myself complain as a kid, and I couldn't get over it. So I talked to other counselors, to prevent the same person from hearing me complaining.

Even though I had started going to counseling, I still felt extreme pain from losing my only brother. However, the pain was not as constant after I had received some pointers from my counselors. I knew nothing could take the pain away, but talking with intelligent people, who cared about me helped. My counselors gave me better alternatives to dealing with my problems. They also taught me better ways to control my thoughts. I learned that the ultimate answer was turning to God. He is the main source of strength that I need to overcome any hardship.

Turning to God changed my perspective on life. It gave me hope. It didn't take the pain away completely, but it was definitely a great help. I realized that the grief that came with losing my brother was going to be a process to deal with. It was going to take time. Nothing would instantly take the pain away. That it would never go away completely.

I still woke up every morning with a bad feeling in my stomach. I still thought about my brother all throughout the day and night. I still had trouble sleeping most nights. But depending on God and talking with my counselors helped me feel better. They also gave me hope. Hope that one day I would be able to mourn my brother and still live. Hope, that God would take care of the person responsible for taking my brother away. I honestly don't think I would be alive today if I had not made the decision to get help and turn to God.

After getting counseling, and working to get my life back on track; I began to have moments where I was motivated to live again. That was a very big deal because for a while I had no hope. I didn't want to live. I woke up every day asking God to take me. After my brother was murdered everything else began to fall apart. I was back living in Springfield, miserable with all the negative around me. But again I held onto God and the spiritual counseling. It kept my spirits up. It changed my life.

After going through counseling I was finally able to go back to church. I had tried to attend a church service after losing my brother, but I couldn't sit through it. The fact that everyone in my church knew about my situation was bad enough. They would all watch me and ask how I was doing. I appreciated their concern, but I wasn't in the mood to talk. I didn't feel like speaking on my brothers' situation. The members harassing me was bad enough, hearing the music was even worse. As soon as I heard the soft music playing, it instantly broke me down to tears. The music reminded me of the music that was played at my brothers' funeral. I couldn't hold it in. I couldn't take it.

After the first incident, I was afraid to go back to church. It was too much to deal with. But after expressing my concerns to my counselors, they gave me pointers of how to overcome those feelings. I prayed about it, took their advice and was able to push through it.

The Moment I Had Been Waiting For

I had gone to the child support office to make a payment. As I'm walking in I notice two sheriff officers in the parking lot. There was usually only one officer, but for some reason two of them were standing out front. I honestly believe it was a sign from God because I was in for the surprise of my life.

I walk into the office, and there is a group of people sitting on the right side of the room. I look over and see a younger guy holding a baby. I don't know what it was, but something seemed strange about the guy. I noticed a feature on his face that stood out to me for some reason. I knew I had seen it before, but I couldn't figure out why it was bothering me. It started to frustrate me because I knew that I saw this person before. Then it hit me! It was Dennis! I had seen pictures of him, but I had never seen him in person. He was actually lighter in person than what he looked in pictures.

As soon as I realized who it was I got this extreme boost of adrenaline. I became angry. I desperately wanted revenge. I had stayed up for hours, every night for the past year, thinking about what I was going to do to the coward who shot my brother. And now I might have a chance to get revenge! I didn't want to kill him. I knew I could not kill a person anyway. My conscience would never let me live that down. I didn't have a problem hurting badly though because I wanted him to suffer.

My plan was to catch him alone. I would follow him, catch him getting out of his car, and attack him. I planned to beat him furiously. Then once I had knocked him unconscious, I was going to break his spine. I sat and thought about it for more than a year! I couldn't believe I was standing close to him after waiting all that time.

I wanted him to suffer for the rest of his life. I wanted him to live the rest of his life in a wheelchair. To never walk again. I wanted him to feel the pain I felt after he killed my brother. I knew I would never be the same after I lost George. I wanted him to be broken the way I was.

But I could not do it there. That really frustrated me. I knew that if I had jumped on him, the workers would call the sheriff who I had just seen standing right outside the door. I figured I would get myself killed by one of the sheriff, coming in to break up the fight. They would most likely pull their guns out and use them. And as much as it frustrated me I had to wait.

But there was no way I was letting him get away that easily. I quickly jogged to my car. I then drove across the street and waited for him to come outside. I wanted to see what kind of car he was driving. That way I could follow him and see where he lived. I knew he carried guns with him, so I couldn't just run up and fight him. I had to wait it out. Timing was everything.

I ended up waiting across the street for more than an hour when I noticed that he called for backup. I saw two cars pull up. I then watched three guys get out, and walk into the child support office. They then walked him to his car and followed him home. One car drove in front and one of them drove behind him. I tried to follow them without being too obvious, but they got away.

I was very, very frustrated about him getting way. It took me hours to calm down. I thought about that day for months! I regretted not jumping on him there. I was very disappointed in myself. But thanks to God I would eventually find better ways to deal with my anger and frustration.

As mentioned earlier, I was frustrated for not jumping on him at the child support office. However, looking back on the situation I had to admit that I was letting the situation control my life. I could've easily gotten myself killed or ended up in prison trying to take things into my own hands. I learned that God will handle the situation much better than I could anyway.

Justice Served

About six months after my brother's death we received excellent news! Dennis had been incarcerated for a driving charge right after the situation occurred. Meanwhile we were trying to put the pieces together to prove he had shot my brother. We had heard different stories about a young man named DJ being involved in the situation. It had been said that the bullet was meant for DJ and my brother happened to be in the crossfire when everything had taken place.

To be honest, I was looking for DJ. I wanted to harm him for putting my brother in that situation. If he had not been near my brother, that whole situation would have never occurred. I wanted revenge and I was determined to catch him sooner than later. But God interfered. My mom had gotten him to testify against Dennis. DJ agreed to testify saying that my brother was an innocent bystander and the bullet was really meant for him.

He held his end of the bargain. He met with authorities and testified against Dennis. His testimony was recorded and ready for trial. It was then reported that Dennis was to be indicted on murder charges! We were still hurt, but it was good to know we would get some closure. But our celebration was cut short. Very short! Somehow his testimony ended up on Facebook! The whole world knew who testified! Two days after he met with the police! By Friday, DJ was shot and killed! I could not believe what had taken place in such a short amount of time.

I immediately called a friend who was an experienced lawyer to ask if his testimony would stick. He advised me that by law, the testimony could not stand because he was deceased. I instantly went into a rage, hearing that news! We were so close! How could this coward get off?? I was hurt and frustrated about the terrible news.

After feeling devastated, I forced myself to pray. I had to put my faith in God and lean on Him for strength. I prayed for justice and God delivered! Two years after my brother's situation, Dennis was caught by U.S. Marshals in South Carolina. He was sentenced to twenty-two years in prison for gun related crimes and shootings he was involved in!

CHAPTER 18

Born Again

I HAD BEEN training friends and family on how to lose weight before the situation had occurred with my brother. But because of that situation, it was difficult to function like a normal person. I could not perform the duties of the job, professionally at that point. So I stopped training. But after completing the counseling sessions, I slowly started to get back to myself.

Coincidentally, my brother was one of my first clients. I knew that he would not want me to give up on my goal. So I decided to go for it and pursue a career as a personal trainer. Meanwhile I was working on my own body by working out and eating healthier. Working out, training other people, and staying busy was another form of therapy. It was a distraction from everything I was dealing with.

After showing results of my own transformation, I eventually built up my clientele. I then created a Facebook business page and continued to grow my business. After that, I knew I had to make things official by getting my certification to train. I found a training class in Dayton, signed up, and completed the requirements to become a personal trainer.

Dedication to My Brother

After forcing myself to accept the reality that my brother was really gone, I decided to dedicate my life to him. I made it up in my mind that my brother would not die in vain. It was the only answer I had for dealing with the pain. I could not let George die alone. I could not let my brother's name fade away. Keeping his name alive was the least I could do for my baby brother.

I began to think of ways to keep my brother's name relevant. I sat and thought for hours of everything I could do for George. The first thing I did was create a Facebook page in remembrance of him. A rest in peace page. A page where friends and family could post photos and share special moments they shared with him.

After I created the page I decided to order memorial bracelets and pass them out. I was excited to see hundreds of people wearing bracelets with my brothers' name on it. I felt George would be happy to see so many people representing him.

After the bracelets were passed out I had gotten a couple of memorial shirts made for my brother. But those were temporary fixes to help deal with the pain. Everything made me feel good momentarily, but I needed something permanent. Something meaningful to have of my brother.

So I decided to get my first tattoo. Before my brother's death I never wanted a tattoo. It just wasn't something I was interested in. However, this situation was different. At that point there wasn't anything I wouldn't do for my baby brother. So I decided to try something different.

My first tattoo was a memorial cross with Georges' name on it. I got it on my right arm. I then added two more tattoos a week after. Altogether I ended up getting six tattoos in remembrance of my brother.

One tattoo stood out from the rest though. I had gotten a portrait of my baby brother tattooed on my chest. It took four hours to complete and it was extremely painful. But it was definitely worth it. The pain of the needle was nothing compared to what my brother had gone through. I didn't have a problem going through that pain for George.

Still, the tattoos weren't enough. I had to do something more meaningful for my brother. Something to show what he meant to me. So I decided to put together a peace walk for him. The theme was backpacks and bucket hats. Everyone who participated in the peace walk were to wear those items during the walk. I chose backpacks and bucket hats because whenever anyone had seen George he was wearing either a bucket hat or his gray backpack.

The walk turned out to be a great success. It felt great to see the park crowded with people coming to support my brother. I had also arranged for there to be barbecue, cotton candy, drinks, and I even got a DJ to play music. To top it off my longtime friend Pastor Eli Williams, gave a great sermon to start off the peace walk.

I also, contacted a local bike crew to escort the crowd while we walked the streets. Everything went smoothly. I could not have been happier to see the turn out for my brother. I felt like he was getting the respect he deserved.

The Facebook page, the tattoos, and the peace walk were just the beginning of my dedication to George. I felt like I owed it to him. Losing my brother changed my whole perspective on life. It opened my eyes to a reality I rarely thought about. That situation made it more clear that we should cherish our time on this earth. We don't know how much time we have left, so make the best of it.

I decided to live life to the fullest. Focus on growing as a person. Staying productive and staying positive. My brother was only given twenty years to live, so I was going to live the rest of my life for him. I was going to cherish every positive moment on earth.

My First-Born Son

Through all the chaos in my life I somehow found time to have a relationship. Growing up I rarely trusted anyone. But when I did it was usually a female. I was very selective with who I shared personal information with. I was so used to not having support that I was reluctant to even talk about my problems. I felt like nobody cared so why say anything?

Despite what I was going through, and despite how I felt, I decided to trust another woman. I was down bad and I felt like I needed someone in my corner. She was the one who answered my calls at four in the morning. She was there when I was up all night crying, trying to cope with the loss of my brother. It was exactly what I needed at the time. The problem is I had mistaken support for love. In return for her support she wanted a relationship. She then went from wanting a relationship to wanting to have a baby together.

I knew I was not ready for a relationship. At the same time, I felt like I owed her for helping me through the toughest time of my life. Me not thinking, figured I would hold off on having a baby until I thought we were ready. But she continued to harp on the situation. It had gotten to the point where she would cry if I had not agreed with her.

Her persistence began to wear on me. Initially I had felt like having a baby during that time was a terrible idea. I knew I wasn't mentally prepared to raise a baby. But after having the same argument for months, I started to think about the positive aspects of being a father. I thought about the baby being another form of motivation. Plus, I knew that I would do anything to make sure my kid had a decent childhood. And a baby might be just what I needed to get back focused on living life the right way.

After about ten months of being together, we found out she was pregnant and we were having a son. I couldn't have been happier to find out that I was having a boy. I started thinking about spending time with my son. Things we could do together. He was the motivation I needed to want to live again. I was in love before I even met my son.

Before I had found out that I was having a son I had no problem dying. The idea had crossed my mind frequently after losing my brother. But my son was the motivation I needed to live. I had to be there for him. He gave me something to look forward to.

Unfortunately, my relationship with his mom fell apart. It became obvious that we were together out of lust. And when you do things out of lust you get negative results. We rushed the whole situation and we weren't able to work things out. Despite the relationship lasting only a short while I am very thankful for my son Javon. He saved my life. There were many moments where I felt like I didn't have a reason to live. The loss of my brother consumed my life for more than three years. And if it had not been for God and my son, I don't think I would have made it through.

First Time in a Mental Facility

Throughout my life I had gone through a lot of adversity. So much adversity that I expected everything in life to be a challenge. And after so many years of dealing with crazy situations, I became immune to the problems. I had many years of practice dealing with drama and hardships.

Well I thought I was immune to it until I lost my brother. Losing George changed everything about me. I was no longer the strong-willed person who could keep a straight face when things were going wrong. I was completely broken after losing my brother. I didn't have the energy to deal with any type of drama. I didn't have any fight left in me.

I had completely lost control of my emotions. The smallest disappointment would break me down to the point of tears. When I had gotten angry I would go over the top. And I started to become frustrated once I realized how emotional I had become. Unfortunately, things would only get worse.

After the split up with Javon's mom, she allowed her mom to get between us and keep Javon away from me. That was a major blow considering I was leaning on my son for strength. I needed him in my life. After going through that I took a dive into deep depression. Each day the thoughts of dying, to join my brother began to sound better. At that point, I knew I had to get a different kind of help. I knew it would only get worse if I had continued to put it off. Depression Counseling was always a rough subject for me, but I knew I had to swallow my pride and get help. It was either that or wait until I made a bad decision based off of hurt feelings.

I knew that one bad incident would take me over the edge. And with me being so emotionally fragile, there was no telling what I would do. I didn't want to be that person. I didn't want to be considered crazy. So I had to put my pride to the side and get the help necessary to help me get back to myself.

Once I had spoken with a counselor in the mental health facility, the psychiatrist diagnosed me with post-traumatic stress disorder. She explained that I was experiencing symptoms of a person who was severely depressed after dealing with a traumatic event. The counselor advised me that by law they could not release me under those conditions.

To my surprise I would have to stay overnight in the facility. The thought of it was intimidating, but I also knew it was necessary. So I put my faith in the counselors and gave it a try. Since I was not allowed to leave I had to call my mom to have her bring some of my belongings.

The whole process was weird. I felt very uncomfortable answering the questions. I didn't like doing the check-in process. I wasn't allowed to bring any sharp objects or use my cell phone because I was considered a threat to myself. I had to be checked by two different doctors to ensure I didn't harm myself every twelve hours. Those things bothered me because I was not suicidal. I never thought of harming myself. I expressed that I had thought about dying to join my brother because the pain of dealing with his loss. There is a difference of being suicidal and being tired of dealing with a traumatic event.

The worst part of my stay in the mental facility was being locked in there with people who had more serious psychological problems than what I was experiencing. Most of the other people in the facility were suffering from severe mental health disorders. Some were drug related disorders, hallucinations, and even schizophrenia. That was very difficult for me to deal with. It was something I had never seen before.

I was determined to get out of the mental facility as soon as I could. The problem is I had to prove I was mentally stable before I could be released by the doctor. But the doctor didn't come in until 6:00 pm. So I knew I would be in there until the following night.

I was starting to feel worse by the minute. They forced me to take medicine. And anyone who knows me knows that I hate taking medicine. Then getting a shot at five in the morning for anxiety made me feel worse. With those two factors to go along with seeing the other peoples' conditions, I decided that I would do my best to get out of there as soon as possible. The feelings of depression, anxiety, and stress were continuing to build up. I just wanted to be alone.

After a long day in the facility, I was able to speak with the doctor the following night. I told him how I was feeling and that I wanted to go home. I also explained to the therapist that I believed the facility was actually making me feel worse.

Luckily for me, the therapist was able to confirm that I was functional enough to leave the facility. He prescribed some anti-depressants and told me that I would be released the next morning. After leaving I was required to follow up with a counselor to make sure I wasn't having any more thoughts of dying. As soon as I was released I got in contact with my spiritual counselor/friend, Pastor Eli Williams and started counseling with him again.

CHAPTER **19**

Pleasant Surprise

I HAD BEEN dating a woman from out of town when I received some news that turned my world upside down. After being together for about seven months, she informed me that she was expecting. The news was surprising because she had told me that she could not conceive. Her doctor had advised her that her hormones were out of whack and that the chances of her getting pregnant were very slim.

Me being stupid, not fully protecting myself, took her word and took a chance. That led to us having a baby together. Having a kid was not the problem. It was the fact that we were not married and I really did not see a future with this woman. I had promised myself that I would not have any more kids until I was married. I also wanted to wait a while until I had another baby. Then to make it worse, I had just gotten baptized. So not only was I dealing with personal guilt after being careless, but I had to hear it from my spiritual family about the terrible choice I had made.

I felt awful about the whole situation. I remember walking into my counselors' office with tears in my eyes because I knew it was going to be rough. I was not in love with this woman, but she was having my child. I felt like I was stuck. I did not know how to deal with that situation. But after months of praying I was able to come to my senses and focus on the baby.

However, the problems did not stop there. She immediately started having complications with the pregnancy, bringing more stress to the situation. We discovered she had a disorder called *preeclampsia,* a disease that could harm the baby. Then after we had gotten that under control, her doctor informed us that the baby was a high-risk for being born with disorders including: autism, cerebral palsy, and many other diseases. It was a stressful time to say the least.

Even though we had enough to worry about, we were still having our disagreements throughout the pregnancy. It was a very, very stressful time. I didn't know how to deal with the whole situation. I just tried to keep the baby in mind. I just wanted to be there for the baby. So I tried to block everything else out.

As time went on, we found out we were having a baby boy. I was excited to find out I was having another son. Someone I could mold into being a responsible, respectful young man. Just the thought of my newborn son bonding with Javon brought joy to my life.

However, the complications continued throughout the pregnancy. The preeclampsia was getting worse along with the scare of the baby being born with disabilities. I was scared out of my mind, but I consulted with my spiritual family and continued to pray about the whole situation. I knew that leaning on God was the only way to deal with the situation.

I remember it was November 2, 2017, I was extremely tired because I was having trouble sleeping. I had been sleeping on the small hospital bed for weeks after she was admitted for high blood pressure. I had only been to my house once in that time period and that was to grab some clothes. I was literally living in the hospital room. I would wake up, get dressed, go to work, come back, shower and sleep on the couch. Wake up the next day and do it all over again. The problem was, it was very difficult to sleep. The conditions, along with the scare of the baby being born unhealthy was driving me crazy. So I decided to take a Benadryl to help me sleep.

I could not have picked a worse time to take the pill. The following morning, I was awakened by a team of nurses barging into the room, rushing her out to the delivery room. They advised us that she would be having an emergency "C" section because her blood pressure had spiked out of control. I was so tired and out of it that I had laid back down after they left, not realizing what had just taken place. After I realized what had happened, I immediately jumped up, put on the robe, and ran into the hallway. I then ran into the nurse who led me to the delivery room.

I remember praying that everything would go smoothly. I prayed that God would interfere and ensure that we would have a healthy baby boy. I had faith in God, but I was still afraid. Plus, this would be the first time that I would witness one of my kids being born. I was not able to see Jayda or Javon's birth. I was scared out of my mind!

But as usual, God came through! **Jerin Dominick Cooper** was born at 7:58 am, on November 3, 2017, weighing five pounds and five ounces! It was a great feeling to hold my newborn baby boy! Holding my newborn son caused me to forget about everything that had taken place during the pregnancy. I was just happy he was born healthy! I'm very thankful God helped us through that situation.

CHAPTER 20

Looking Back

I HAVE BEEN dealing with adversity since the minute I came in to this earth. And I am sure there will be more tough situations in the future. I was born into chaos, but God brought me through it. God, along with the strong mind he blessed me with would not allow me to give up.

It wasn't pleasant growing up the way I did. My biological father and my mom split up when I was born. And my step father was no example for me to look up to. I grew up looking stupid, being ignorant to the basic mannerisms of a how a young man should act. I learned everything through trial and error.

I was forced to learn from my own mistakes. I was clueless to simple things such as: a man's role in a family, how to represent myself as a responsible person, how to deal with adversity, how to treat a woman, and even the proper way to show emotion. I had no idea how a father and son should interact with each other. But as I got older I told myself I would continue to get better. I learned things by watching people around me and looking back on my own mistakes.

I suffered from low self-esteem for years. I didn't think anything of myself. I was always confused. I was clueless. And whenever I made a mistake, the people around me laughed and made fun of me. Instead of showing me what I was doing wrong. They didn't give me advice on how to correct my mistakes. So I was forced to grow up quick. I also realized that I would have to fend for myself.

I remember being envious of kids who had fathers in their lives. A father to teach them, protect them, and show them the way. I envied people who had families who stuck together. People who genuinely cared about them. I envied them because I didn't have either. And to be completely honest, it hurt. It hurt to come to the realization that I didn't have a loving family. I would have to grow up without support.

But after a while I stopped feeling sorry for myself. I told myself I was going to be a decent person despite the hand I was dealt. I always had moments of self-doubt, but I refused to stay down. I set goals for myself that separated me from other people around me. I refused to be just another delinquent coming from the streets of Springfield. Even though a lot of people doubted I would become a decent person. But I didn't care what other people thought about me. I had my own goals in mind. And I wasn't going to let anyone stop me from reaching my goals.

I set out to be different, prove the doubters wrong, and leave a positive impact on everyone who ever knew me. At the same time, I wasn't afraid to be my own person. I wasn't afraid to stand out from the crowd. And even in my lowest moments, my moments of battling depression I refused to be a bad person. I have made plenty of bad decisions especially out of anger, but I am far from a bad person. I have always wanted to be a decent person and I am still working to be better today. My mission is to face my flaws like a man and learn from mistakes. To be willing to do whatever I have to do to get closer to God. And I will be a great father for my kids. Those are the things that motivate me.

I have accomplished goals that I doubted I would accomplish. I would be lying if I said it came easy. I would be lying if I said there weren't times I wanted to give up. But I have learned that trials and adversity are a part of life. Everyone has to deal with some form of adversity. The problems don't make you it's how you respond to those problems is what makes you.

I have lived in homeless shelters; I have gone to bed hungry on numerous occasions. I have asked God to let me die so I could join my brother in heaven. I have been ridiculed by those who say they love me, lied on, talked about, and forced to stand alone at a young age. But still! I refuse to quit. I refuse to punk out. I refuse to stay down. I refuse to be a statistic. I'm still learning. I'm still growing. And I will continue to get closer to God. I will continue to survive and I will continue to move forward!

To everyone else I was just another poor kid with no future, coming from a broken home. I would end up just another drug dealer, or some kind of low life stealing from people or hurting people. But God had other plans. Plans for me to be somebody. And I am very grateful for everything God has done for me. I am grateful to be able to have met so many people, to have traveled to so many places, and accomplished what I have accomplished.

I worked hard to separate myself from the negative things I grew up around. It took extreme discipline and determination. It would have been easy to follow the crowd and pick up on the things that were going on around me. It would have been easy to give up and sell dope. I could just blame my parents and my excuse be that I grew up around it. But I thank God that I didn't. I know God placed a basketball in my hands for a reason. Playing basketball took me away from the things that would have resulted in my demise. Demise of my character, my spirit, and even my life.

Playing basketball took me away from the troubles I was facing in my personal life. Playing ball allowed me to see the world. People respected me because of the things I could do on the court. And I'm proud of that. Nobody can take that away from me. And once I got closer to God I knew there was nothing anyone could do to defeat me. I have been through hell, but I'm still here. **Still Standing**!

Throughout my life I was hard on myself. I was hard on myself because I wanted to be different. I didn't want to be like other people I grew up around. I refused to make excuses for the mistakes I made. I refused to put it on other people or ignore my own issues.

Looking back, I can honestly say I am proud of who I am. I came from Springfield, Ohio (voted the most miserable city in the United States) and went on to graduate from the College of Wooster (ranked in the top 50 best colleges in the United States).

Who would've ever thought? They told me that I had no chance of graduating from college because my parents dropped out of high school. The enemy told me I could only dribble a basketball. That I wasn't smart enough to graduate from one of the top schools in the country. But God said I could! And I did! I'm thankful that Coach Moore and Rodney are genuine people who cared enough to help me get through college.

I was blessed to be able to travel across the United States playing basketball. And I did it free of charge. My hard work and dedication on the basketball court made it possible. I never would've been able to afford to travel and play in those tournaments if I was not an exceptional basketball player. If my coaches and sponsors had not stepped in to help, I never would have left Springfield. I thank God for all of them. They had faith in me. I sincerely appreciate everything they have done to help me.

I was very fortunate to have the opportunity to visit cities such as: Las Vegas, Beverly Hills, The Bahamas, Paris, Los Angeles, Chicago, New York, Florida, and many other exciting places. And the only reason I was able to visit those places is because of basketball. I got a chance to play on ESPNU, and be filmed by a live television camera (a childhood dream of mine). I can now tell my kids that their father was once a professional basketball player. I can encourage them to shoot for the stars. And if dad can do it, they can accomplish much more. And I promise to give my all to help them reach their goals and dreams.

I finished my basketball career at Wooster winning more awards than any other player in school history. I also set many records in both school and conference history. I was fortunate yet surprised to make the conference all-decade team. I was also notified that **I will be being inducted into the College of Wooster Hall of Fame on September 21, 2018**! I am looking forward to bringing my sons Javon and Jerin with me to experience such a positive event. It will be a memory I will never forget.

Overall I accomplished a lot even though I came from nothing. And I want my readers to know that if I can do it, they can too. No matter your background, how poor you are, or where you come from. God has a plan for you and it's not to fail. Follow God, believe in yourself, and there's nothing you can't accomplish. Everyone isn't going to support your dreams. In fact, most won't, but those people are irrelevant. The only opinion that matters is yours!

CHAPTER 21

The Aftermath

TODAY, I'M BETTER than I have ever been and I owe it all to God. If I had not turned to God, I would not be the person I am today. I'm sure I wouldn't be alive if I had not turned to God. I also want my readers to know that I put a lot of effort into writing this book. It wasn't easy letting my feelings out. Certain situations were very difficult to talk about, but I wanted my readers to get the real story. To experience the toughest times and some of the best times of my life with me.

Losing my baby brother knocked me all the way down. Down to the point of wanting to die, anxiety, severe depression, and many other psychological problems. I was at a place where I thought I would never recover. I didn't see any hope for the future. But God put some people in my life who really cared about me. Those people picked me up. I am still hurting from losing my brother. I will never be the same, but I know I have God on my side. I can't lose.

I also want to make it clear that I have made plenty of mistakes in my life. I am not above anybody. I am far from perfect. I will not blame anyone for my mistakes because it's nobody's fault but mine. I have done many things that I am not proud of. However, I will not allow my mistakes to define me. I made a promise to myself to keep trying to get better. To not accept mediocrity. To never stay stagnate.

My way of dealing with my flaws is to own up to them. To learn from my mistakes. I'm learning to give my problems to God and allow Him to help me. That alone has changed my whole perspective on life.

I am now living mostly guilt free because I have confessed my sins and I know God has forgiven me. Yet I still have more to learn and plenty of growing to do. I am not a victim. I am a survivor.

I am very fortunate to have my son Javon in my life, and I am working on getting custody of my daughter Jayda, who is in Colorado. It has also been a blessing to be able to spend time with my youngest son Jerin. I am enjoying every moment of time I have with my sons, but I also need my daughter in my life. Through it all I am working hard to stay positive about life. I am focused on positive things that have lifted my spirits up.

Spending time with my Javon has turned my world around. I get to be the father I always wanted as a child. I can't wait to get Jayda back, and spend more time with my youngest son Jerin. I love my kids more than life itself. I still struggle at times though. Sometimes, I look at my son and I wonder why my dad left me. I think about the fact that my father never played with me as a kid. How he missed so many important moments in my life. And sometimes I get stuck in this depression mode.

But every time I get down God brings me out of it. He helps me focus on the fact that I can be the opposite for my kids. I fight it off by turning to God and focusing on positive things. I'm more than ready to be that loving, caring, supportive, father I needed when I was a child. And I will work as hard as I can to be that type of father for all of my kids. My kids mean everything to me.

I will never be a perfect father, but I promise to continue to try to be the best father I can be for them. There is nothing more rewarding than being a father. Investing time into your kids. Trying to mold them into being children of God. I hope and pray that I can create a special bond with all three of my kids. They are everything. I will do everything in my power to guide them, love them, support, encourage, and protect my three. I will put my life on the line for them. I love you Jayda, Javon, and Jerin. I'm nothing without you!

To add to the positive aspects in my life, I was baptized on **February 19, 2017!** I always knew I wanted to get baptized, but I put it off because I was nervous. I was worried about being held more accountable by God for my actions. I was not sure if I could change. But I am very thankful I took that leap of faith. It is one of the best decisions I have ever made in my life. I feel like a new person because of it. Now I have to continue to seek God and work to be a better man. Javon being present at my baptism made it a hundred times better! That is the type of example I want to set for all of my kids.

As of today, I am focused on being the best man of God I can be. My personal life is fine. However, I have distanced myself from my family. We grew up in a harsh environment to say the least! My brother is gone. My sister Darrien is currently serving six years in prison for an incident with her son. But to her defense, she was not mentally stable when this had taken place. My sister was suffering from post-traumatic stress but nobody would support her. Only one of my sisters has graduated high school. We grew up fighting amongst each other instead of being taught to bond together. Yet my parents feel like they didn't play any part in this. It's crazy but I have to step away. I still pray for them but I can't keep my sanity and deal with them at the same time.

I also want my readers to know that I am just the opposite of what everyone expected of me, and I am proud of that! I grew up in the projects, the very bottom. But I not a street guy and I will never be a thug. In fact, I hate drama. I don't want to be involved in anything negative. I'm a firm believer that you can overcome trauma from growing up in a broken home. And just because you come from the streets doesn't mean you have to act street. I mean that and I stand on that! I'm proud to be living off of my own vision and not from what other people expected from me.

Career Wise

I am blessed and very grateful to be working with the youth of Springfield, at InsideOut! It is an organization that is built around leading our youth to Jesus while also providing care for those who come from broken homes. I am working as the youth director. My job is to be the example of the person who grew up in the same environment, but did not fall victim to my surroundings. To help them understand that we cannot live a successful life if we do not include God in it. I am blessed to be in a position to be able to do something I love and call it a career.

I came from a broken home and I have personally experienced majority of the hardships our youth have faced, so to be able to work with them and give them the blueprint to overcome their circumstances is like a dream to me.

My Parents

I mean this from the bottom of my heart. This isn't coming from anger or frustration. It is coming from years of examining my life and looking at facts. But in my heart, I believe that I was born to the worst parents a person can ask for. And I honestly believe that. I catch myself wondering why they ever had kids. Both my mom and dad are extremely selfish. My dad has every excuse in the book for why he left me. He takes no ownership for us meeting when I was thirteen and not having a relationship today. He puts it all on my mom.

My mom has done some really foul things. She lied to me about not receiving child support for twenty-four years. She put bills in my name when I was a kid. And she recently asked me to help her with a title loan that would help her pay her rent but only made one payment on the loan. I lost my car in the process and she refused to pay the money to me so I could get another car. But by the grace of God, I found a cheap car within two weeks.

Those two weeks of not having a car sent my stress levels through the roof. And to be honest, I did not see a way out. I spent my time walking, stressing, not knowing if I would be able to buy another car at all. I was also unable to pick my boys up. Which lead to other arguments from their mothers.

In all honesty, no one on this earth has gotten over on me the way my own mother has! Nobody has let me down the way my father has. I don't remember ever getting encouragement from either of them! Instead I was told I thought I was better than my family whenever I came home from college. But its ok. It motivated me to push even harder!

Through everything that has taken place between me and my parents, there is no hatred. Just lessons learned along the way. Through the hurt and pain, they made me stronger! They pushed me to want more out of my life. And I thank them for that.

What I Am Most Proud Of

As a kid I didn't think I had a chance to be successful at anything. I always doubted myself. I never felt good enough. I woke up stressed every morning scared of what the day was going to bring. And to be honest, I felt that way because I did not have support at home. I was constantly yelled at for any and every thing. Then I had to go out into the world and deal with angry, immature people.

My mom literally beat me down with words so bad that it destroyed my confidence altogether. I never thought I would be good at anything. I was mentally defeated before I had even started any venture. No matter if it was school work, sports, or even trying to be a decent person. Which is why I've never been good at accepting compliments. I didn't think anything of myself so why would anyone think highly of me?

But through all of that **I am most proud** of being able to deal with my rough upbringing and keep my composure. By the grace of God, I've been able to hold it together. Most people don't have a clue of what I have gone through because I never allowed my circumstances to dictate my personality. I thank God, I was still able to find motivation from within. I thank God I was able to stick to my own plan and not allow other people to get me off track.

I still struggle with some things, but I have gotten much better at controlling my emotions. I'm working on dealing with moments of weakness. I still get random flashes of my brother in my head. Then I think about my kids and how I will die before I let them feel the way I felt as a kid. I never felt loved by my parents. That's the honest to God's truth. Never! But even in my weak moments, when I feel like I'm worthless, I get angry and fight back. I will never give up. It hurts but I have to find a way to beat those feelings. I have to! There's no other way. I will keep fighting until I beat that mindset.

Those who have read my story have asked me how I did it. They ask how I was able to deal with the things I dealt with without losing my mind. And my answer to that is, God saved me. He blessed with a strong mind. A stubborn personality. I didn't want what everyone else wanted. I didn't care how bad life was, I wasn't going to follow behind anyone else or use my circumstances as an excuse to do bad things.

Purpose of This Book

My intention of writing this book was to inspire, and hopefully motivate someone who is going through a tough time. I want to give hope to people who are battling depression the way I was. I want to give hope to kids who are being told they will never amount to anything. I want to give hope to those who were born poor, and don't see a way out of it. I want those kids to know that they can achieve any goal and overcome any obstacle life throws their way.

I wrote this book to inspire others to be great. To let people know that even though you can't choose the hand you are dealt, you have a choice of how to play that hand. We all have choices in life. You can either take the blows and keep pushing or allow your problems to consume you.

I want people to know that you have to fight to survive. Just make sure you fight in a positive, constructive way. Make sure you are fighting for something that matters. You have to separate yourself from the pack. It won't be easy, but it is definitely possible!

Be different! Stand out! Rise above! Set your own goals. But know that it all starts with God! With God on your side you can do anything. Stay productive, stay positive, and always remember to put God first.

My Goals

My goals today are: to include God in everything I do, to continue to work to be a better man every day, find a career that allows me to do God's work, help others, to be the best father for my kids, provide a nice, safe home for them, teach my three to be better people than what I am, to honor my brother, find peace in life, and avoid anyone who brings negativity into my life. Life is too short to be angry, stressed, or unhappy. I just want to live peacefully.

Sometimes, I sit and visualize, what I am going to teach my kids when they get older. I am going to shower them with love, support, and encouragement. I'm looking forward to picking them up from school and asking how their day went. I get emotional just thinking about my kids asking me to help them with schoolwork. I get emotional thinking about creating positive memories with them. I even get emotional thinking about my kids playing ball. I can't wait to teach them how to play. I feel confident that they will be better ball players than what I was. But even if they choose not to play sports I am going to love my kids regardless.

Thank You's

I would like to take this time to thank everyone who has had a positive influence on my life. I appreciate everything you guys have done. I would not be the person I am today if it wasn't for you guys. First and foremost, I want to thank God for everything. God has stuck with me and He has blessed me with wisdom, courage, good health, and a strong spirit. He has also placed some very influential people in my life. I want to **thank God** for giving me twenty years with my baby brother, Little George.

My brother made a hell of an impact in just twenty years and I am proud to be his older brother. My brother inspired me to want to be a better person, because I knew he was looking up to me. I knew I had to set a positive example for him to follow. I would like to thank my **Grandma Quick** for being a positive inspiration to me and for teaching me morals. She was the first person to encourage me. She truly believed in me and it helped my confidence tremendously. I would like to thank my spiritual counselors for giving me the positive word of God and leading me in the right direction. For taking time out of their busy schedules to listen to my problems and complaints. I would personally like to thank **Glenwood Davis**, **Dan Cecil**, **James Penrose**, **Stephen Massey** and my cousin/Pastor **Willie White** for everything you guys have done for me. You have no idea how much you have affected me and pushed me to become a better man. You guys have given me hope in a time where I felt hopeless. I would like to thank **Pastor Eli Williams** for investing in my life for the last twenty-two years! You have counseled me, taught me how to serve God and changed my outlook on life. Thank you! I would like to thank **Mr. O'neill** and **Mrs. Sullivan** from Catholic Central for giving me lunch money when I was a student at Central. You guys have no idea how much that helped me. I would like to thank **Mr. Larry Baker** for helping me through high school and through college. You have helped in more ways than you know. I want to thank **Yelvis Parker** for being my coach, my mentor, and giving me a place to live when I was in the seventh grade. I am still grateful that you opened up your home to me. You were like a father-figure to me. I want to thank my cousin **Danielle Harper** for taking me in after I lost my brother. I would like to thank **Susan Samuels** for giving me my first coaching job. And for helping me, and guiding me along the way. Mrs. Samuels has been providing support for more than seven years now. To this day, she stills give me advice on getting ahead. I would like to thank my good friend **Rodney Mitchell** for everything he has done for me. Rodney, is the most down to earth person I have ever met. Thank you for helping me get through college. I would like to thank my best friend, a person I have been knowing since I was seven years old, **Isaiah Carson**. We have been through a lot together and we have grown so much as men. I would like to thank my great friend **Kyle Wheeler** for everything he has done. Kyle, has helped me in many different ways, and on many different occasions. You are appreciated. I have to thank my friend **Manny Plataniotis** for giving me a place to stay when I was down and out after losing my brother. I would like to thank **Coach Steve Moore** for recruiting me, and giving me a chance to play college basketball. You were much more than a coach. You were a great mentor. Coach Moore is one of the most genuine people I have ever met. I would like to thank my good friend **Larry Doyle** for all the help, and advice. For opening up your home to me when I was down. I would like to thank **Stephen Massey** for the mentoring, and the guidance. For taking time out of your schedule to counsel me and uplift me. You have helped me in more ways than you know. I would like to thank **Mrs. Teresa Parrett** for praying for me and allowing me to find volunteer work. Mrs. Teresa is an excellent person who loves to help others. She puts a lot of time and effort into her soup kitchen and food pantry, serving others. I would like to thank **Pastor Bill Stout** for allowing me to work with the youth and believing in me. Thank you for all you do for the youth in Springfield. I would like to say a special thank you to Mr. **Glenwood Davis**. You have worked miracles in my life. You have given me advice, and helped me in ways that I could never repay to you. I would like to send a special thank you to **Dan Cecil**, and **Glenwood Davis**, for teaching me about God, and helping me get my life back in order. Glenwood Davis and Dan Cecil are truly angels on earth! Thank you guys. I would also like to thank any and everyone who has said something positive to me or about me. I want to thank everyone who helped me become the man I am today. I appreciate everything you guys have done. I love you all. Thank you for putting up with me. Thank you for allowing me to be me.

CPSIA information can be obtained
at www.ICGtesting.com
Printed in the USA
LVHW010541130720
660475LV00003B/155